CONSUMING HOPE

FATHER AND SON AND FOUR DAYS TO LIVE

RYAN FASANI

PRAISE FOR CONSUMING HOPE

"[Ryan Fasani] bears witness to the profoundly good news of divine presence manifest in weakness, redemptive forgiveness made possible through vulnerability, and an eternal love that is stronger than the abyss of death itself. As soon as you enter this story, powerful currents of longing, grace, and ultimately assurance of the precious goodness of life will quickly carry you through and remain as gifts of sustenance that you'll long remember."

— TIMOTHY REINHOLD EBERHART
Leiffer Associate Professor of Public Theology and Ministry, Garrett-Evangelical Theological Seminary

"Consuming Hope washes over you like a prayer. And like prayer, the journey of connection to the Divine comes from unexpected revelations. Few authors are adept enough in piercing their own vulnerability in a way that invites you to willingly and gracefully do the same. Fasani touches on a subject that every human will experience; but what makes the journey worth it is the beautiful intersection of storytelling, faith and theology, pain, and transformation found within this book."

—ERIC PAUL
Executive Director, West Hawaii Mediation Center

"This book is authentically Ryan Fasani in all of his intelligent, risk-taking, non-conformist glory . . . sit at his feet and learn from him. He is a man who thinks deeply, takes risks, works hard . . . and points people in the direction of God."

—DAN PALMER
Ex. Director, Youth for Christ

PRAISE FOR CONSUMING HOPE

"It is clear that God soaked every part of Ryan's journey with goodness and grace as he found himself accepting his father's diagnosis, journeying through his childhood emotions as an adult, and feeling release with death. Ryan didn't walk readers through from a pastoral perspective because that would be too obvious. He walks readers through the collision of grief and hope from the place of a son. I read this book in a day because I couldn't put it down. It captivated me in a way that awakened parts of my soul that still needs to experience reconciliation, healing, and hope."

—ANH JOHNSON
Lead Pastor, New Legacy Lynden
Customer Success Manager, FaithLife

"I was completely drawn in to this story of grief and hope. Ryan tells a story which is remarkably specific and yet I felt my own wounds being healed the more I read. I was surprised at the depth of Ryan's reflections. His profound insights reveal an uncommon experience with pain and contemplation. This book invites you to journey far beyond the counterfeit "solutions" for sadness to a deep-rooted, long-lasting, and life-giving hope."

—NATHAN OATES
Lead Pastor, Emmaus Church Community, CA and author of
Kingdom Come: Seven Ways to Experience Resurrection Here and Now

PRAISE FOR CONSUMING HOPE

"In Consuming Hope , Ryan Fasani takes us on a journey through a dark season of connection and loss. The treasures he uncovers are not necessarily what we expect to find. And somehow in Ryan's touching vulnerability, we're empowered to reexamine our own stories.

—JAYSON D. BRADLEY
Pastor and Patheos blogger

"Rare is the writer who is able to keep us riveted to his central story while, at the same time, addressing inescapable theological and philosophical questions raised by that story. All of Ryan's training and experience in ministry were sifted like wheat in the encounter at the end of his father's life. He comes through it chastened, humbled and liberated to love more deeply. Consuming Hope is a gift to anyone willing to honestly reflect upon their own faith and relationships."

—RICK POWER
District Superintendent, Church of the Nazarene

"Intimate, contemplative, and beautiful, Ryan's travelogue of an Emmaus Road of grief explores the textures of the language of weakness and mortality for a culture that lives in denial of its limits, and finds by dwelling in that shadow the transformative compassion of Christ and the real possibility of a redemption we experience in our mortal bodies even in the face of death."

—THE REV. NATHANIEL OGDEN KIDD, PhD
Reconciliation Anglican Church, Bellingham, WA

To Dad,
for being strong at the end.

To Mom,
for massaging Dad's feet even when he couldn't feel it.

"I want you to walk with me to the end. I trust you will go slowly. I don't want to go fast. I want to ask questions."

"I can't promise I have many answers, Dad. But I can promise that I will tell them straight, and I'll tell you when I don't really know."

"I just want you there with me."

"Okay, Dad. Okay."

CONSUMING HOPE

FATHER AND SON AND FOUR DAYS TO LIVE

Ryan Fasani

CONTENTS

PREFACE
CONSUMING HOPE

What you hold in your hands are tear-soaked, tattered notes from Dad's bedside. It all began by accidental adventure into the mysteries of a life lived largely in secret. These pages were *not* planned, *not* formulated at a desk, beginning as an idea, then an outline, and eventually a manuscript. That's too formulaic, too clean and simple. These notes were jotted down through tears and snot and shaky hands—the unglamorous result of exploring Dad's wounds and regrets and fears.

I ended up on this journey with Dad in the same way that kids accidentally wind up on forest adventures. They begin with a little wild curiosity and a tiny bit of courage to take one step beyond the tree line. That first step is to look into the shadowy understory beyond the clearing, and the next step is into another land, another vegetative world of exploration and discovery. I was curious, so I took the first risky step into the shadows of Dad's life. The rest of the adventure that is now this book was initially me trying to keep up with my discoveries. I took a lot of notes along the way!

What a child finds in the wildness of the forest is not foreign but native land, for all children have a bit of primordial wildness in them, defiantly resisting the sanitized, controlled environments to which they are subjected to day in and day out. Nor did I find what I was discovering in Dad's final days of life to be completely foreign. The end was terrifying and traumatic, but I was drawn in by an ineffable familiarity that resisted platitudes and simple explanations. Within me was a brokenness that found a home in my father's brokenness. I deeply connected with Dad's suffering, the darkness of Amyotrophic Lateral Sclerosis (ALS), and the darkness of untold stories that Dad clenched and held close.

After Dad died, the adventure continued. The notes turned into journal entries, which turned into reflections of how some journal entries connected with others. I was writing to make sense of my writing and to make sense of my forest discoveries. But I also was leaning into the grief and exploring my own shadows and theological questions. What began as a risky adventure into my father's darkness became a season of grief and self-discovery.

This story was going to get written one way or another. I had a wild story that wanted out. This is a story about how light was found through an accidental adventure into darkness. It's a story about how life can be discovered beneath the underbelly of suffering and death. It's a story about ALS, about death, but it's also a story about hope.

Admittedly, this story is still tear-soaked and tattered. It still reads a bit like field notes. It's still an adventure.

Ryan Fasani
March 2020

INTRODUCTION

The miraculous is not extraordinary but the common mode of our existence. It is our daily bread.

              — *WENDELL BERRY*

Two buildings are emblazoned with his name at Wilson C. Riles Middle School: "MARK V FASANI." A cast bronze plaque at the entrance of one building attests to his reputation as a teacher. A firm handle on classroom management, steady leadership, and staff room humor define his legacy on campus. The buildings are monuments to his teaching career but are veneers over the truth of his private struggles.

Dad was handsome and brilliant and humorous. He stood tall with dark curly hair, icy blue eyes, and wore just enough of a smirk to show how handsome he was and how little he tried. He was disciplined and well groomed, a perfectionist without leading on to his obsessions. He was articulate and astute without a hint of pomp. By all measurements, he was successful, full of self-assurance and confidence. However, his physical traits and social grace hid a life lived mostly in secret.

I watched my father in the final few days of his battle with a torturous disease. In those final hours of vulnerability, he shared openly, and I learned the great contradiction of a man he was. He was tall and strong yet struggled behind insecurity and loneliness. He was gregarious and witty but was afflicted with depression, detachment, and doubt. He cherished his family, devoted to meeting every need, but he couldn't emotionally connect. He was a father and friend, coach and colleague, teacher and mentor, but he was racked with darkness and hurt, and harbored anger and anxiety.

But it was also in those last days, when the illness had taken its course and ravaged his body, that the man hidden from his colleagues, and even from his family, had emerged. On the final stretch of his journey, with no buildings and plaques to hide behind, when Dad was the most physically frail, his soul smiled and hope was most evident. It was there at the end, in his brokenness, that he taught me just how close the Divine is.

It was a rare treat to see my father smile.

Dad smiled before and after fulfilling his dream of taking Mom to Switzerland. He smiled when all five of his sons graduated college. But sometimes a smile is so genuine and free it unlocks the sobering grip history has on one's memory. I recall two scenarios when Dad's smile and laughter was just so pure and genuine. The first was Dad on his Kubota tractor, and the second was at our dining room table.

"Dad, you're on that tractor every day."

"Need to move some material . . . gotta move material, Ryan."

The truth is, Dad was on his tractor because that was where he was the happiest, driving in circles, pretending to move dirt. Sitting atop his shiny new toy with a big smile on his face, his hands on the steering wheel, ready to take flight. Unfortunately, ALS took that Kubota tractor away from Dad and that smile disappeared.

The other memory of that liberating smile and laugh, which is really a collection of memories, is of my father sitting at the head of the dining room table. The only thing that rivaled the Kubota tractor in giving Dad joy was at dinner was family meals abundant with wine and warm ciabatta bread. ALS took the Kubota, but it wasn't getting the bread and wine! We can say that Dad went out in good form—perhaps not physically laughing, but certainly his soul was smiling. The last decision he made was to enjoy a bit more wine while bread was set on the table.

The Road to Emmaus is a story of two brothers in the throes of grief and lost hope after the crucifixion of Jesus. On their walk home, they befriend a stranger and eventually invite him to stay for meal. The story culminates with the return of hope over a meal.

Khubz, or pita, is at the center of that meal; without it, the rest of the food items are disparate dishes. The bread, essential but never the focus, humbly works to tie all the other dishes together into a collective and filling meal. Dad's final four days of life are the focus of this memoir, but without bread, all the respective pieces will seem disparate and disjointed. The

Emmaus bread serves as an adhesive to hold all those parts together.

Bread is also used as an edible utensil. It is torn and used to dip, scoop, or pinch substance from another dish, and then consumed together. The process is not clean or uniform by Western standards. No edges are straight, and no two pieces of bread are the same size. But when utensil and dish are combined in an edible vehicle, the mouth awaits a delicious combination of flavors. I will tear pieces off the Road to Emmaus bread, dip them into portions of Dad's story, and consume them together. As a warning, this will not be a clean process. I'll likely make a mess, but the hope is that the two stories will merge and become something delicious.

The Emmaus journey ends in the very place where Dad fully enjoyed himself—at a table, set with bread and wine. In both stories, bread becomes sacred, and daily bread becomes miraculous.

After my father's death, I was off-balance, disoriented, and wrestling with unjustified loss. I needed to grab on to something, talk to someone, grieve, and make sense of the trauma.

The Road to Emmaus story became my dialogue partner. Often, we need to say what we think so we can discover what we really believe. In other words, we need to "talk out" our feelings, hunches, and thoughts as they relate to an event, and in the very process of articulating those impulses, we discover what's underneath them. This requires a dialogue partner that is particularly good at listening and perhaps even better at directing our attention to what we might be missing.

The Emmaus story "listened" to me "talk out" the complexity of my experience and pointed me to new discoveries. Every time I revisited the story, I would find more of my dad, myself, and the infinite variabilities of our stories intersecting with Luke's story of lost hope and its return. The Emmaus story also did something else.

I was looking to understand and find meaning in my father's suffering, and I wanted to put some of the pieces back together from my own head-on collision with death. Unfortunately, I didn't find the meaning I was looking for because suffering is inherently devoid of it, and I'm still broken into pieces. Thanks to the Emmaus story, I did discover something deeper. Under the pain—in the confusion, darkness, disorientation, and mystery we all feel in suffering—I found a deep hope.

This story is not about discovering the meaning of death as much as it is about Dad's story bearing witness to a deeper hope in all of our stories of suffering. It's as much about my father as it is about me discovering more about myself. The journey for me continues, and I hope it prompts you to discover meaning on your own journey.

THE ROAD TO EMMAUS

LUKE 24:13–35

Now that same day two of them were going to a village called Emmaus, about seven miles from Jerusalem. They were talking with each other about everything that had happened. As they talked and discussed these things with each other, Jesus himself came up and walked along with them; but they were kept from recognizing him.

He asked them, "What are you discussing together as you walk along?"

They stood still, their faces downcast. One of them, named Cleopas, asked him, "Are you the only one visiting Jerusalem who does not know the things that have happened there in these days?"

"What things?" he asked.

"About Jesus of Nazareth," they replied. "He was a prophet, powerful in word and deed before God and all the people. The chief priests and our rulers handed him over to be sentenced to death, and they crucified him; but we had hoped that he was the one who was going to redeem Israel. And what is more, it is the third day since all this took place. In addition, some of our women amazed us. They went to the tomb early this morning but didn't find his body. They came and told us that they

had seen a vision of angels, who said he was alive. Then some of our companions went to the tomb and found it just as the women had said, but they did not see Jesus."

He said to them, "How foolish you are, and how slow to believe all that the prophets have spoken! Did not the Messiah have to suffer these things and then enter his glory?" And beginning with Moses and all the Prophets, he explained to them what was said in all the Scriptures concerning himself.

As they approached the village to which they were going, Jesus continued on as if he were going farther. But they urged him strongly, "Stay with us, for it is nearly evening; the day is almost over." So he went in to stay with them.

When he was at the table with them, he took bread, gave thanks, broke it and began to give it to them. Then their eyes were opened and they recognized him, and he disappeared from their sight. They asked each other, "Were not our hearts burning within us while he talked with us on the road and opened the Scriptures to us?"

They got up and returned at once to Jerusalem. There they found the Eleven and those with them, assembled together and saying, "It is true! The Lord has risen and has appeared to Simon." Then the two told what had happened on the way, and how Jesus was recognized by them when he broke the bread.

I

CRUCIFIXION

*[They] handed him over
to be sentenced to death,
and they crucified him.*

— LUKE 24:20

PHONE CALL

It began with a phone call to North Idaho in September.

My family owns a piece of property on the bank of the Moyie River, thirty miles north of Bonners Ferry, Idaho. That is to say, we have a cabin in the middle of nowhere. The cabin is generally used for vacationing, but I moved with my wife, Bohdana, and our four children to live there permanently in September 2015.

I'm the fourth of five sons, no sisters. My father and mother, both teachers and coaches, raised us playing sports, working hard around the house, and excelling in our studies. We were taught that with enough effort there were no limits on what we could accomplish physically and scholastically. My observations of my older brothers supported that lesson.

My oldest brother, Rick, lettered in three varsity sports and led his Academic Decathlon team to back-to-back California state championships. Of the many Ivy League schools, Rick chose Dartmouth College. Rob, my second oldest brother, followed in

Rick's footsteps and headed East to study engineering at Dartmouth. Rick played volleyball, Rob played rugby, and both maintained a very high GPA. The third brother, Randy, was a scholarship athlete at Stanford University and eventually played in the NFL. Rocky, my younger brother, was also a 4.0 scholar athlete, excelling in basketball and football. He attended a liberal arts university in San Diego and set his eyes on a respectable career in firefighting.

I didn't attend a prestigious institution or become a professional athlete, but I still pursued dreams with the same intensity. And, thanks to my parents, I believed there was no ceiling to my potential. Until there was.

I'm a minister by training, and for fifteen years I served in the local church as a youth and young adult pastor, compassion ministry leader, and senior pastor. During that same time, I completed graduate school, planted several churches, developed a network of food banks and urban gardens, and traveled as a speaker.

I eventually ran out of steam while pastoring a church on the Big Island of Hawaii. Moving to Idaho was an admission that I had limitations. In the summer of 2015, I finally accepted the truth that trying to pull myself out of exhaustion only compounded the weight I carried. I moved to Idaho because I simply couldn't go on another day without deep rest. I was physically and mentally spent. I was spiritually empty. I was a shell of my former self.

So we moved from Hawaii to the cabin in Idaho in September. The mornings were cool, and winter was itching to settle in the small valley at the base of the Purcell Mountains. We moved six thousand miles, unpacked our moving container, and experienced our first freeze in years, all within a couple days, all while wearing flip-flops and swim trunks. Without boots and only a hand-me-down sweatshirt from my older brother, Rick, I was unprepared for the cold weather.

My mother came up from California to lend a hand. We worked hard that first day. There's a long list of to-dos to properly winterize a cabin in the middle of nowhere in North Idaho. We stowed away hoses and garden tools, blew out water lines, organized the outbuildings around the property, pruned shrubs, and cleaned out flowerbeds.

Mom loves to work with her hands and stay active. Her short gray hair is the only thing that leads on to her age. The bounce in her step, her toned arms, and her love of manual labor make it hard to believe she's any older than half her age of sixty-eight. No one who knows my mother well would be surprised if she requested to be buried in her blue jeans, favorite gloves, and a garden shovel.

My father would have joined her in helping us, but he was ill. For almost a year, my father had one doctor's appointment after another, but no one had been able to give a name to his symptoms. His appetite waned and he had lost weight. His six-foot-two frame resembled that of a distance runner more than the muscular, former high school running back. Thin and exhausted, Dad could manage most personal, daily tasks on his own. The demands of housekeeping, cooking, and taxiing to doctors appoints was too much. For the first time since Rocky, the youngest of the five brothers, lived at home, Mom was a caretaker. She needed a vacation, and our move coincided with a break between doctors' appointments.

My mother jumped on a plane alone, but she *did* bring Dad with her in the form of worry. I noticed it most when she would stop working unexpectedly. While coiling a hose, for example, she'd stop and stare across the field, not looking at anything in particular.

"Mom, what are you looking at?" I asked, trying to align my eyes with hers.

"Nothing. Just thinking about your father. I hope he's okay."

There was so much familiar about Mom's trip: the chores, the traveling alone, her work ethic. But her worry was unfamiliar and ominous. It carried within it a subtle foreshadowing, as if her intuition insisted on her being ready for change, ready for the unfamiliar to permanently break into the familiar.

The second day of Mom's trip was different.

I'll never forget the morning the phone rang. I was in the kitchen, boiling water for coffee. My children were sitting with my mother at the dining room table playing cards and talking about the moose Mom spotted walking across the front lawn. Bohdana was frying eggs to accompany the pancakes. Despite the sunny sky, autumn was in full swing, the maple leaves were changing colors, and we were all content with our progress from the day before.

The phone rang. It was Dad. Mom answered with a nervous tone, "Hey, Mark!" She dropped her chin, closed her eyes, and paced back and forth across the kitchen, clearly trying to process the weight of my father's words. "Oh no. No, no, no," she said before walking into the next room in search of privacy. Hearing only my mother's side of the conversation for those few seconds before she left the room was enough to assume the worst.

"What should I do, Ryan?" Mom asked when she returned to the kitchen.

"Well, what did he say?" I asked, only half wanting to know.

"He said he was lonely. And he said he's not feeling well."

"Anything else?"

"Yeah, he said he's panicking a lot and can't stomach food. And he's relying on the walker and still having a hard time getting around."

"Is that all?"

"He said a lot, but it was hard to hear him. He's not just lonely, Ryan. He's desperate."

Mom is an optimist. I've learned that to get an accurate portrayal of any event or experience, I need to divide the positive in half and multiply the negative by three. In this case, the result of the equation was clear: Dad was in terrible need of help.

"You need to go, Mom. First thing in the morning."

She agreed and booked a flight. Early the next morning, she headed back to California to attend to Dad's needs.

THE JESUS MOVEMENT began with the public speaking of another man. In the deserts and fields of first-century Palestine, John—in the tradition of the Hebrew prophets—rebuked sin and admonished the Jewish people to return to a radical life of piety. He was a simple man, living with little more than a message for God's people.

But John's message of repentance came with a special level of urgency. He was preparing the way for the coming Messiah, the Savior of Israel. He called for repentance of sin; he called for washing clean the filth that tarnished the uniqueness of Yahweh's chosen people. John the Baptizer preached that a literal washing would usher children of Israel into a new era of God's people. While John spoke with confidence, he lived with conviction and humility. He had the posture of one not worthy of touching even the filth on the feet of his successor (John 1:27).

Dad's phone call was a type of John the Baptizer moment—it was a precursor to monumental change for our family. John was the precursor to Jesus, as he prepared the way for the one who would eventually prepare an altogether new way living in and experiencing the world. The phone call was a forewarning of events that would altogether change the way my parents would see and hear this world.

John announced a new era that would hold in it death and new life, judgment and redemption. Dad's phone call was an announcement of a new time in our family that would also include death, life, judgment, and redemption. The phone call announced a new future, a future *in the present.* The call foretold a future full of limitations, suffering, and hopelessness. The call itself didn't announce something coming, per se, but pointed at a time that had already arrived. My father was desperate and suffering and yet his disease was still undiagnosed.

Like John the Baptizer's announcement, the foretelling *was part* of the new era that was coming, which is to say that the future was already present but still emerging. It extended far beyond John but included all of John's work. He didn't so much warn about tomorrow but instead put different parameters around what constituted "tomorrow." Tomorrow included today. The future was here, but only in part.

The entire year was marked by Dad's increasing weakness. My parents were so hopeful despite the evidence. Unwavering was their belief that a prescription would reverse the tide of weakness and weight loss. They firmly believed that a proper diagnosis and effective medication were around the next corner, after the next appointment, with the next expert.

Together they hung on to the belief that better days were ahead. In a way, the power of their hope for healing was simultaneously a weakness. It inhibited their ability to prepare for alternatives. My parents' imaginations were colonized by a promise of better days. They were subservient to a team of doctors, who themselves were subjects of a broader medical system. No one is to blame for implanting the sound bite, "Better days are coming, better days are coming," but it was their shared anthem, and it played on repeat. The concoction of a high trust in modern medicine, inexperience in physical suffering, and a general sense of disempowerment was a recipe for being controlled. Each ingredient played an essential role in the power their misguided hope wielded over them.

My parents needed to believe that things were going to improve. To imagine anything different was not within the scope of possibilities. Psychologically, this optimism is powerful, even helpful. But when the test results had no findings, the medications had negative side effects, and there were many nights without sleep, the only way my parents could manage was to believe in better days ahead.

I didn't share in their hope, but I couldn't blame them for having it. This is what we do as humans to try to cope—we cling to any sort of hope, even if it's just a sliver. But their unwavering hope also served as a type of denial, which was a major hurdle in preparing for the worst days ahead.

But crisis chips off a piece of denial, and continued crisis cracks right down the center, allowing the truth to seep in. John the Baptizer served as a continued crisis for the Roman Empire, offering a contrast to the promise of peace delivered by Rome. He baptized people into this new reality, causing a hairline fracture that was soon to burst into a pronounced fissure and a break from oppression. His message was part of the new reality, the break from the old.

My parents' hope for healing, which served as a denial of the truth, was structurally weakening. The crack was made, and their imaginations were opening to the possibility of different outcomes.

Their new reality had arrived but only in part.

The complete shattering of hope would come.

Soon they would fully realize that Dad would never heal.

2

AUTUMN

OCTOBER, NOVEMBER, AND DECEMBER WERE DARK, SLOW months. My father was weak in a way that no one had ever seen him and no doctor could explain. He slouched, shuffled his feet, and mostly talked in a whisper. Every activity was exhausting and yet the cause of his decline was still undiagnosed.

Whenever I'd talk to Mom on the phone, I'd always ask how my father was doing. She'd often say, "Dad is sicker this week," or, "He's weaker today," or, "He's moaning right now." She'd tell me about Dad's migraines, panic attacks, and his loss of appetite. Every time she tried to explain Dad's condition, she'd include a type of verbal onramp: "You're not going to believe this," or, "It's the weirdest thing." Those onramps caught my attention, mostly because they were unnecessary and unhelpful. I'd wonder, *Why not just say it straight, Mom? Why the warm-up? Why the unhelpful phrases?*

Sometimes the unhelpful onramp would be more lengthy. "Well, you know," she'd begin, "your father's never been like this. It's just not normal. I can't explain it, but it's like nothing I've seen. I try to tell him to do this or that, and he won't listen. But even if he tries and does exactly what the doctor says, he's still not himself. It's the weirdest thing." And then she'd say stuff like, "He lost five more pounds this week and can't keep his anxiety in check."

It occurred to me afterward that Mom's verbal onramps, though unhelpful to me, were necessary for her. They were *Mom's* onramps, her way of easing herself into the delivery of bad news.

I'd also ask about her own well-being. "Mom, this must all be very hard on you. Are you taking care of yourself? Are you doing okay?"

Usually it was the same response: "Yeah, I guess I'm doin' fine." Except for that one time—and it was only one time—when she said, "Ryan, I'm exhausted. Dad never sleeps. I mean, I really do like taking care of him, but I'm just tired. I'm going to need help."

"That's perfectly normal, Mom—"

"But I don't want a pity party," she interrupted. "I don't need a pity party."

Something wasn't right. *Was it the tone in her voice? Was it her word choice?* And then instantly, like a motion-sensor light, the sensor tripped, and I could see what was right in front of me.

A pity party.

That phrase tripped the motion-sensor light. Her verbal onramps caught my attention, but I couldn't put my finger on why. Now I could. It was that little phrase I'd heard so many times growing up: *pity party.*

Weakness. It was all about weakness!

There's nothing to dislike about pity. It isn't something that's intrinsically negative or harmful. One may listen and be sensitive, or be sympathetic and express sorrow in my situation. These responses are not inherently bad. However, *pity* is the word my family attributes to sympathy or compassion when we don't feel we are deserving to receive it. It's not that we're averse to sympathy; it's that we don't want to be the kind of people who *need* sympathy. We ostensibly ascribe the word *pity* to what we receive from others, but really it names something *in us* that is triggered when we receive compassion.

If we are comfortable being weak, we welcome the gift of sensitivity and call it sympathy, compassion, or some other word that truly names the concern of others. On the other hand, pity names the discomfort we have when our weakness is shown to us. If our weakness is something that is downright unbearable, my family calls it a "pity party."

I learned at a young age to not seek pity. When I was eight, I split my foot wide open climbing on rocks in my backyard. The gash was big enough for at least a dozen stitches. No ER visit, my mother propped me up on the kitchen counter, dug out the gravel that was lodged in my open flesh, and flushed the wound with hydrogen peroxide. I squirmed and wailed as my mother pinned me to the counter until the burn wore off.

"We'll put some tape on it, and you can use the crutches tomorrow for school," Mom instructed.

"What if it starts bleeding in Mrs. Lake's class?"

"You can wear two or three socks on that foot. No one needs to know."

"What if it hurts really bad? What if I can't walk to recess and they want to send me home?"

"You'll be fine. Don't make a big deal about it and no one will pity you."

My mother's attempts to explain Dad's dwindling health revealed that my family finds weakness downright unbearable. We have literally built a paradigm of toughness around us, a world understood through the filters of stability and strength. Consequently, we never developed a rich reserve of words to accurately express our pain and weakness.

Mom didn't have the words for Dad's pain. I didn't either, but I knew that pity was not it.

My mentor was fond of quoting German philosopher Ludwig Wittgenstein: "The limits of my language mean the limits of my world."[1] What Wittgenstein meant was that the potentiality of his experience was governed by the language he approached it with, and his understanding of experience was limited by the words he could access to describe them. It is reasonable to say that the language we have, or better yet, the language we allow ourselves to access, puts limits on how we experience the world.

We needed a better way of talking about Dad's sickness so that we could open up to the true depth of pain and weakness—both his and our own. Only then could we cultivate the eyes to see and ears to hear the truth about Dad's condition and our future. We literally needed to burn down the paradigm of strength we had grown so accustomed to—and all the language that supported it—if we were to share in Dad's hurt.

Life is not merely defined by competition, as if we're beasts in the wild trying to survive, nor is it up to pure chance, as if we float through life and wait for events to bump us. We are participants in the nature of life, never totally in control but sometimes totally controlled by it. But life is seasonal and cyclical, and there is familiar movement to it. As I searched for new language, the metaphor of seasons, specifically autumn, was helpful to understand the changes we were experiencing.[2]

Autumn at 7110 Baywood Lane—the house I grew up in, and the house where Dad was ailing—is marked by signs of both dying *and* explosive life. On one hand, the flowers begin to droop. The frost inflicts pain on the hanging pots first. They have less protection than those that are shielded by ivy or hedges of bushes. The droopy color fades and soon will be given back to the earth as compost, the roots bearing down for the colder nights ahead. The Liquidambars offer seed pods that speckle the driveway like earthly goosebumps.

On the other hand, the leaves put on a dazzling show of arboreal fireworks. Almost boastfully, they compete for attention—some yellow, some red, and some orange. The Japanese maple leaves turn a heavy red, its bending arms offering the leaves as a type of early wrapped Christmas gift to winter. The bare ground from the dry days of summer reveals a storehouse of grass seeds that sprout as the temperature cools and the moisture promises to stay. And somewhere between the dying and living are the oak trees that stand their ground, holding strong to their color and form, but even they sacrifice acorns to the changing season, littering the ground with squirrel feed.

Autumn is the season where the life of summer and the death of winter collide and the sparks of color fly. Darkness is near; death is waiting its turn. But the business of summer is not quite finished. The sun's energy packages all of its warmth and growth into small seeds. Autumn receives the summer seeds with one hand and holds back freezing winter for a couple months with the other.

Everything seems to fall, but not without purpose. Leaves fall but will become the mulch to protect the soil from winter's harsh frost. Nuts and seeds fall, and they'll become spring's great rise and summer's big growth. Inevitably, though, fall is a fall toward death.

In early October, Dad called Mom to help bear his pain. He summoned her in the heart of autumn, literally and metaphorically. His body was ailing, drooping, atrophying. He was rapidly losing weight and fighting daily threats of migraines. He was suffering from anxiety attacks at an unprecedented rate, and the frequency of doctors' appointments and trial medications triggered both the anxiety and the migraines. Nights were sleepless and days were draining. Everything seemed to be falling. Winter's death was creeping closer.

That autumn for my father was marked by life and death with beauty somewhere in between. For the first time in either of their lives, one was severely ill—experiencing a true autumn. The life and growth of the previous season was slipping away and it would not return until the far side of winter. Dad was weak, tired, seeing the darkness of winter closer than ever before but unwilling to let go of summer.

In their last year together, my parents had to renegotiate their relationship. No more summer trips to Home Depot or long days on the tractor. Dad needed help, and he was dependent on Mom.

It was beautiful.

In the collision between their former marriage and the end of life—between summer and winter—was an autumn of real beauty. Their marriage took on the colors and splendor that could only happen in the chilly air of fall when winter threatened to take over and the stored energy of summer refused to give in. Seeds of love dropped, ready to be received by the patient soil of life and marriage.

The ministry of Jesus was a type of autumnal season in the life of Israel. When he began his public ministry, he was sandwiched between a growing awareness of Israel's redemption and the threat of incarceration and death. In the collision of those two seasonal pressures, life abounded. The beauty of autumn shone itself before the defining death of winter. He bore the seeds of a new Kingdom and planted them anywhere they'd be received. Those seeds would have to hunker down for a season, but they were full of all the energy and the DNA necessary for spring growth.

THERE ARE two seasons in North Idaho: wood-chopping season and wood-burning season. Having moved from Hawaii, wood-burning season began the day we arrived. I spent many hours chopping and hauling wood and building and stoking the stove in the corner of the cabin. It also meant I got to enjoy the natural heat as I peered out over the Moyie River that ran through the property.

I was beginning to appreciate the slower manual chores of living in the mountains. I noticed vitality returning. I was finally resting after all those years of sprinting in ministry. As snowflakes began to fall that November, I realized it was the first holiday in fifteen years I would be without pastoral responsibilities.

Ironically, a pastor is the most frazzled and stressed during seasons of focused worship, celebration, and merriment. As people slow down and spend time with family and friends during the holidays, a pastor's schedule swells with obligations and responsibilities. My daily existence was a sharp contrast to that dynamic now. And I felt full.

A peculiar emptiness came over me as Thanksgiving approached. My entire family usually gathers at my childhood home in California for the holidays. As a pastor, my work schedule was usually in conflict with these family get-togethers. In years past, our absence didn't bother me so much, as I considered it a small consequence of following my vocational calling. But that holiday season it did.

Perhaps the intentional season without ministry gave me time for introspection. I finally had time and space to look within, which had a way of helping me see the values that have been lost in the periphery of life's busyness and ministry's inconvenient schedule.

Perhaps I reached an age or life stage marked by sentimentality. Late at night, I would flip through mental photo albums of my family sharing turkey and stuffing, elbowing each other on the couch during the football game, wearing big, hearty smiles. I think it was a bit of all those things . . . but there was something more. Something else was drawing me home. Something deeper seemed to be tugging at me. It was something about my father.

My father's concern for me was always a concern for my material well-being. It was pragmatic and stale. He never told me that he thought of me often or that he was proud of me. There was no connection of that sort. Instead, when I was a boy, he'd ask about my homework and grades, game schedules and sports gear, the flat tire on my bike, and if my chores were finished. When I was an adult, he asked me about investing in retirement, oil changes and tire rotations, salary and career plans, the HVAC system and water heater, and if I patched the leaking roof.

I always wondered if Dad loved me. If love can be considered a space in us that we reserve for an other, I assumed he had a small space for me. His concerns seemed obligatory. Our pragmatic relationship was another box to check on his weekly list of things to do. I craved finding space in his heart that was wide and expansive. But it just wasn't there.

I was never intentionally distant from or resistant to my father; I just didn't have a lot of room for him in my heart either. The best I can describe it is that my capacity for loving him was never cultivated and therefore never grew.

When I was a child, I would go days, sometimes weeks, without talking to my dad. He was up before all of us boys, and I'd only see him before he grabbed his briefcase and hurried out the door to work. The same image but in reverse—hurrying inside and putting down his briefcase by the backdoor—was often the only time I'd see him before bed.

My time of introspection while in North Idaho helped uncover a truth I mostly overlooked. I learned that I had a low receptivity to different forms of love. I had a Bundt cake mold for love: it was shaped a certain way, and it needed to look and taste and smell according to my expectations for me to delight in it. I began to understand Dad's love for me, and I mostly missed it because I was expecting something else, something he was not able to offer.

My father's expression of love was not by any measure an emotional connection, but it was indeed love. He expressed it in the best way he knew how. He never once warmly bid for my attention or told me he spent hours thinking about me, but his questions did. All the talk about flat tires, homework, salaries, and roof leaks were a testament to just how much time and energy he actually devoted to me. My Bundt cake mold was shaped differently, and so I missed it all.

Dad worried about me often in the way only a father worries about a son. No one else asked me about my bike because no one else worried about me crashing while riding on the trails around our home. No one asked me about changing my oil because no one else imagined me stuck on the side of the freeway. The same is true about jobs and benefits and retirement. Only my father stayed up at night worried sick that I'd be stricken by a huge financial burden.

Dad worried about me because he loved me and he cared for my well-being. That's it. There was no paternal cheerleading or heartfelt emails, no birthday cards or affirmations. My father worried, and I was learning that worrying was his way of loving. And something emerged in that autumn, while living in North Idaho: I learned to see and receive Dad's love.

It wasn't a rational decision, as if I gathered enough evidence and convinced myself to see paternal love; rather, the sensation was more internal, more from within, more at my core. It began in my stomach, and I can only describe it as a capacity, a space waiting to be filled with Dad's love.

The more I understood Dad's shallow questions as signs of deeper love, the more the capacity within me to love him grew. Being loved—even if that love was always there and I was only just beginning to notice it—birthed within me the capacity to love. Or being loved begat love within me.

It was the first holiday season I was not swamped with pastoral responsibilities, I was finally resting and becoming noticeably more sentimental. More than all those influences, it was my father's love that was drawing me home. The more I was able to recognize Dad's persistent love, the more I changed. That change was most evident deep within me as a type of internal draw, an internal longing to be back home. I wanted to reciprocate that love. I wanted to express my appreciation for his pragmatic concerns over the years, be present with him, worry with him, love him in return.

3

DIGNITY

As November turned to December, winter settled in on Idaho. The ground was covered with snow, and the garden was put to sleep until spring. Wildlife was noticeably less active and quieter, and the serenity of the cabin was a delight. The predictable rhythm of our days and the natural beauty were healing for my soul. We were ready for winter.

In contrast, my father's health was plummeting. He was gaunt and his anxiety attacks seemed increasingly severe. The whole month of December, while much of the world prepared for holiday celebrations, Dad and Mom suffered through medical appointments and sleepless nights. And then, in a type of unexpected medical blizzard, on the morning of Christmas Eve, my family received a diagnosis that froze us in our unpreparedness.

I'll never forget the empty silence when my mother called. I answered the phone and there was nothing. I said "Hello?" a second time, and again got nothing. Just as I was about to hang up, a quiet voice, shaky and full of trepidation, said, "Ryan, I wanted to call you before I send an email to family and friends. Your father has ALS."

"Oh my God . . . oh no. No. Mom, I'm so sorry."

I clenched the phone hard and sobbed.

My father, sixty-nine years old, was diagnosed with Amyotrophic Lateral Sclerosis (ALS) the morning on December 24, 2015.

Let me be blunt: The diagnosis is a death sentence.

There are three things that are known for certain about ALS. The disease is named after Henry Louis "The Iron Horse" Gehrig, the famous first baseman for the New York Yankees, the cause of the disease is unknown, and there is no cure. In other words, we don't know very much.

In 1938, Lou Gehrig, in his sixteenth year as a Yankee, began losing strength. His statistical prowess as a leading hitter in Major League Baseball faltered, and though he still played above average, he was noticeably weaker than the year before. Early in the 1939 season, Gehrig, weak and slow, benched himself after starting 2,130 straight professional games. A few months later, June 19, 1939, Lou Gehrig was diagnosed with ALS.[1]

The *A* in ALS stand for *amyotrophic*, which comes from the Greek word that literally means "no muscle nourishment." It's a disorder that inhibits communication between the motor neurons in the brain and muscle cells.[2] The muscular system suffers from a slow degeneration, eventually resulting in a complete loss of voluntary muscular movement. While the initial symptoms are difficult to detect, eventually muscle begins to severely shrink, speaking becomes slurred, swallowing becomes a challenge, and breathing is impaired. The autonomic nervous system, however, is generally spared from negative effects, which means ALS patients often maintain the ability to hear, see, touch, smell, and taste.

The disease creates an unbearable dichotomy, one in which the suffering patient becomes a witness to his or her own inabilities. The body begins to die, but the mind and sensations are active and alive. The patient is split in two: mentally standing on the sideline of their own losing match, sensing all the agony of dying without the physical abilities to respond. It happens slowly, torturously, as the average duration of ALS is three to four years.

The medical field—that modern day behemoth of science and medicine—is supposed to have omniscient capabilities . . . or at least that's our expectation. We admit ourselves into hospitals, submit ourselves to experts and their tests, and expect objective, measurable results. ALS defies this expectation in that it is the diagnosis that is given when all other diagnoses are ruled out. It's not diagnosed, per se, it's deduced as the final option. In other words, my parents learned that ALS was not the conclusive result of many tests; it was all that was left when there were not conclusive results. The diagnosis began to seem a lot less scientific and a lot more subjective.

When my father was officially diagnosed with ALS, we had so many questions that had no answers. Where does ALS come from? Is it preventable? Why didn't it show up on any tests over the last year? How do we know for sure that it's actually ALS?

"We really don't know," the doctors said.

Receiving a diagnosis for a disease that the medical community knows little about is a medical paradox. We were surrounded by medical experts, but none of them knew anything or could answer our questions. It's helpful and unhelpful at the same time. On one hand, the diagnosis was consoling because we could finally put a name to my father's mysterious symptoms. One the other hand, the diagnosis was devastating because the culprit remains elusive and untreatable.

"We really don't know" is the worst kind of answer in the medical field. It's medical code for, "We're at the limit of our abilities." In Dad's case, it wasn't just a death sentence; it was a sentence to die without intervention and help. We could name Dad's condition, Amyotrophic Lateral Sclerosis, but we knew little about it. ALS is a bone-chilling, wintry stumble toward death, and we were unprepared for that blizzard.

BEFORE THE ACTUAL crucifixion of Jesus, he was first "handed over" to the authorities. He was apprehended in the Garden of Gethsemane and put in a Roman prison. The biblical story moves pretty quickly from the garden to the cross. This should not minimize the importance of that experience or the trauma Jesus experienced.

The torture of Jesus didn't begin with his physical beating but with his incarceration. The torture of incarceration—in a Roman prison *or* a modern-day penitentiary—is not the loss of rights or the restriction of freedoms, but is the acquisition of a torturous point of view. That is, the trauma is watching one's own life from the outside while being helplessly removed from it. The diagnosis of ALS meant that Dad would be "behind bars" in his own body.

The dying process with ALS is layered with small deaths along the way. Like other degenerative diseases, the slow loss of physical ability is a dying of hobbies, livelihood, self-care, and independence. And with these "smaller" deaths comes a wake of destruction. The most painful destruction seems to be of a psychological nature—it's the destruction of what could have been, what life ought to have been. Dreams are destroyed, and hopes and desires die.

Dad didn't have big dreams. They were reasonable, conservative dreams to help him wind down the last third of his life. Dad had worked over four decades—tirelessly overworked most of those years—so that one day he might be able to retire, enjoy a few toys, and follow a predictable routine.

He wanted to wake up casually in a retirement home, enjoy his coffee and paper, and consider for several hours how he might put his Kubota tractor to work. Then, by mid-afternoon, he'd fire up the Kubota and move some material from one part of the property to the other. He would wipe the tractor down, come in for a beer, watch a game or two, and fall asleep in his chair.

His dreams were mundane, even boring. But to Dad, they were a perfect balance of work and play—on his terms. The path of destruction laid by ALS was not only killing Dad's motor skills, but his humble dreams and mundane wishes for the future were also dying. For Dad, retirement was freedom and the disease was torturous incarceration, a prison of death.

Death is like a ghost that haunts us the entirety of our lives. It's the boogeyman that awaits at the end of the dark hallway of life.

Theologian Paul Tillich calls death our primary source of anxiety.[3] But death—the ghost—comes in more than one form: physical and existential. The former is the death of our bodies, which causes the anxiety of mortality. We worry that life as we know it, in these bodies, will end. The latter is the death of meaning, which causes the anxiety of emptiness. We worry that this life has no ultimate purpose. We combat the anxiety with the courage to embrace the humanity that is our fleshly, physical existence and find the answers to the questions of purpose and meaning.

But what happens if the death is slow and gruesome? What do we do if the cause of immense suffering and death has no meaning? How do we face it then? This kind of death is the worst imaginable death because it confirms our biggest fears.

The ravaging ALS does on the body cannot be numbed, hidden from, or denied. It forces its victims to come to grips with the bitter truth of humanity. The suffering is without explanation, without purpose, or without meaning. ALS is the supreme ghost of our fears, looming in the shadows, ready to unpredictably and arbitrarily inflict a victim with slow death.

The bodies of the victims of ALS are alienated from the mind. It forces the afflicted to own his or her own finitude, and that finitude serves as a gauge for how far the victim is removed from controlling the inevitable. The victim becomes their own bystander as they traverse the horrific path of suffering.

Crucifixion is not merely the means to end a life; it is a calculated expulsion—socially, culturally, and politically. The guilty party is bound and removed from his or her livelihood, social relationships, religious participation, and political involvement. He is led outside of the city fully exposed, completely stripped of dignity. Crucifixion is fundamentally an isolation unto death, a complete loss of purpose. While the body is slowly dragged toward death, the victim is forced to face the two fears of life: mortality and meaninglessness. In this way, ALS is a crucifixion, a terminal expulsion from one's own autonomy. The victim becomes a withered version of himself or herself.

As my father slowly suffered from loss of control, he said to my mother, "Protect my dignity. Protect my dignity." He knew what every crucified victim learns: slow, torturous death threatens to take away dignity, the holy grail of personhood. Crucifixion intentionally strips one of dignity. It is a war on the body—not to kill it, per se, but to use it as a spectacle of suffering. Death may actually be desired by the victim, but it's a type of sustained living that makes crucifixion effective in robbing dignity. The crucified is a mangled, naked, helpless life, barely sustained in the eyes of the public. The body becomes a banner of humiliation and dishonor.

Dad's fear of his own mortality was augmented because he knew that the crucifixion of ALS could render him alive but helpless, his body barely living, waving publicly like a flag of shame. Protecting Dad's dignity meant helping him resist the physical humiliation that he so feared.

On top of his request for dignity, my father had one other plea. "Don't leave me alone," he repeated to Mom on Christmas Day, less than twenty-four hours after receiving the diagnosis.

While crucifixion is the dismembering of the body, publically stripping people of dignity, it also dismembers the victim from social bodies. Crucifixion eliminates the social nature of people's lives. In other words, when others are needed most, the victim is forced into isolation. Dad couldn't bear the thought of being alone. He feared what we all fear: undignified physical death and isolation.

I didn't talk to my father when my mother shared the news about the diagnosis. After a disorienting and emotional hour, I called to talk to Dad directly. While my four children ate lunch and my wife wrapped the last of the Christmas presents, I snuck away to my office. As the phone rang, I wondered, *What do I say? Is "Merry Christmas" insensitive? Should I ask him how he's doing?*

Mom answered. I could hear her trying to manage her cry.

"Can I talk to Dad?" I asked gently.

I was surprised at my father's ability to not talk about the diagnosis. He asked about my children and the weather and a few other inconsequential issues. I turned the conversation toward the obvious, but the only words I could find stumbled out. "I'm so sorry, Dad."

His response surprised me. "There's nothing else. It's all I can think about, Ryan." He repeated that second phrase three or four times. "Tell Bohdana and the kids I said 'Merry Christmas.'" That was my cue he had enough.

"I'm sorry, Dad . . . Merry Christmas."

Dad's crucifixion was not only destroying his health and inflicting him with fear, but it was also consuming his thoughts. His body couldn't escape the inevitable death. His thoughts were now handcuffed to the same immovable reality. All Dad could imagine was slowly dying. His body, his things, his world were slowly becoming undone.

Josh Stoning, a close friend and farmer (with an uncanny love for compost), introduced me to the idea that "the process of decomposing and decay are often more feared than the moment of death" because it grabs ahold of our imagination in a more profound way.[4] Whereas death is the end of life, decay marks the process of continued death, which is a process of decomposing.

Paradoxically, a terminal disease like ALS is a type of decaying *before* dying. The degenerative process of the body is a living decay, affirming the decay in the future. The very thought of our bodies (and things) decaying is almost unbearable, but the physical experience of decay is downright crippling. All my father could think about was his diagnosis because it was confirmation that a slow and graphic undoing of life was underway. Everything valuable to him will experience the same fate of decay: decomposition, disintegration, and disappearance.

ALS is a torturous concoction. The victim begins to wither away and relationships begin to fall apart. When the diagnosis is given, death is served. The victim's body, livelihood, and social connections decay while a clear mind, without a choice, stands witness.

Like Dad, it's all I could think about.

4

CHRISTMAS

GROWING UP, CHURCH WAS CASUAL. AS A FAMILY, WE PREFERRED contemporary worship over hymns, khakis over slacks, and entertaining sermons over monotone homilies. Appropriately, our church was in a community center with movable chairs and a modern sound system.

However, while the atmosphere was casual and friendly, the theology was rather conservative and staunch. One of our most prominent skills was drawing lines. We drew lines between who belonged and who didn't, between acceptable behavior and unacceptable behavior, between the right and wrong way to vote, and between many more ins and outs. By far the most important line we drew was between those saved and going to heaven and everyone else who was unsaved and going to hell.

Quite naturally, family and friends who had an affinity for our version of evangelical Christianity asked questions about my father's salvation. Some messages came in moments after my mother sent an email on Christmas Eve day with the "crucifixion notice." Her email read:

> What an email to have to send out on Christmas Eve day. I first called [my boys] but now I want the rest of the family to know, including of course my three prayer partners, my pastor, and our best friends, Bob and Susan . . . This morning, the muscular neurologist said that all signs and symptoms are ALS . . . Needless to say, it was a long ride home from Kaiser . . . I have a feeling there's going to be a lot of tears this Christmas.

The questions started arriving within the half hour. Was Dad aware of his sinfulness? Was Dad's soul secure? Did Dad accept Jesus as Lord? Did Dad know if he was going to heaven? Should we pray for his conversion? Did he repent and say the sinner's prayer? While the questions seemed a little abrupt, they were well-intentioned and familiar. And they all shared the same soteriology.

Soteriology is the theological term that refers to the doctrine or teaching of salvation. Every question about my father's salvation presupposed a particular soteriology. It goes like this: Salvation is the saving of one's soul *from* the consequences of sin and *for* eternal life in heaven. With a prayer of confession, hell is averted.

From the standpoint of finitude, these concerns are sensible, even expected. Heaven serves as the antidote to mortality and meaninglessness. Quite simply, heaven is the perpetuity of life. Also, it gives purpose beyond the dark curtain that separates this life from the unknown next one. In other words, heaven is a pearl-studded, gold-laced security blanket for the future.

This concept of salvation, and by extension heaven, offers more than just never-ending life; it addresses our existential relationship to finitude itself. In other words, heaven "deals" with our anxiety around death by telling us, "Don't worry about it."

The questions coming from loved ones were familiar but were they appropriate? Were they the right questions to be asking? The closeness of Christmas, which was less than twelve hours away, demanded I ask. Family and friends were concerned about my father getting to heaven, and Christmas was the holiday that celebrated God's preoccupation with getting to Earth. Those two observations seemed incommensurate.

A perfect example of this idea of salvation is the story of three-year-old Colton Burpo in the book, *Heaven is for Real*. Colton suffered from appendicitis and had an out-of-body experience while on the operating table. Colton literally went to heaven and returned to share his story about it. Among other things on Colton's heavenly journey, he sat on Jesus' lap and learned facts that predate his birth.[1] The book was wildly successful because it capitalizes on the deep-seated fears—mortality and meaninglessness—we have about death. Colton's voyage to heaven confirms the possibility of eternal life, and sitting with Jesus pacifies the anxiety of meaninglessness.

As a miraculous healing story, Colton's testimony is wonderful, but as a story about heaven, it's rather unfortunate. He had to leave his body to visit heaven. For him to get a taste of salvation, he had to leave Earth. This undermines the affirmation of our bodies that is the incarnation of Christ and the possibility of affirming what Jesus called the Kingdom of Heaven. *Incarnation* is a critical word here. It refers to the general concept that there is divine presence within human flesh. Specific to the Christian tradition, it refers to the belief that God took on a human body in the form of Jesus the Christ.

From the standpoint of *finitude*, the evangelical concept of heaven is sensible. Heaven is a good answer to the scary questions about ultimate meaning. "What's the point in all this? Is there a purpose?" Of course! The point is an eternal, utopian destination. And if death is scary, heaven is the promise that it doesn't have to be. Living forever, free of pain and suffering, is an option. This concept of heaven thwarts mortality.

But from the standpoint of the *incarnation*, heaven as eternal bliss (and salvation being the ticket by which we get there) is unreasonable. Incarnation both affirms our finitude and offers an alternative to the anxiety of death. God took on human flesh, mortality, finitude, and suffering. The infinite indwells the finite. The here-and-now is pregnant with heaven!

This is why the incarnation *and* Jesus' mandate to love are antithetical to the concept of heaven promoted by Colton Brando's book and behind the questions about my father's salvation. Love is not a generic mandate that is hollow in practice; rather, it's a firm injunction to step into the very crisis of this world that we would otherwise ignore, repress, or try to escape. The anxiety induced by mortality and meaninglessness has an antidote in this perspective. Freedom is found in the very act of lovingly embracing finitude. In other words, incarnation offers an alternative to escapism, which is at the heart of otherworldly concepts of salvation. Freedom from the fear of death, modeled best by Jesus, can be found by fully embracing this world, this life, and our neighbors.

As evening settled in on our cabin, I tucked the kids into bed, and my wife filled the stockings with goodies. Stuffing stockings is one of my favorite traditions. Christmas music playing in the background, we always stuff until the stockings are swollen and spilling over. We lean them against the presents at the base of the Christmas tree.

But that year was the first time I didn't cheerfully participate. I was consumed with questions about heaven, salvation, and the divine presence. All the questions, however, seemed to trivialize my father's pain. I abhorred trivializing suffering of this magnitude. I wanted to acknowledge it and affirm it. I wanted to embrace Dad in his suffering, not offer him an escape.

Questions about salvation are not befitting the face of suffering and dying. They are not only inappropriate, but they quite possibly undermine the very intent of asking the questions in the first place.

We ask these questions because we believe that it will save the dying from the fear of death by promising life in heaven. But this often accomplishes the opposite. Our anxieties have such a powerful influence on us that in the presence of someone else's finitude, we can force those fears on the dying without knowing it. We thrust our own anxieties onto the person through the guise of our "concerns about their salvation," disregarding whether they have those same concerns or anxieties. Instead of bearing witness to an alternate reality without fear, we make fear the defining framework of our relationship with the suffering individual.

In addition, rather than affirming the fact that in suffering there is the presence of the Divine, we desire seeing a conversion—a saving of the soul for eternal life in heaven. Unfortunately, through desiring this type of salvation experience, we expose our disbelief in our own "belief."

Remember, salvation is a type of escape to heaven where God is present, omnipotent, relieving all worries and pain. But the belief that death and anxiety is ameliorated in the very presence of God is suspect, insofar as that experience must wait for death itself to arrive. God is not exclusively in "heaven by and by." It seems clear that concerns for a *salvific* (admittedly a nerdy term that means "of or relating to salvation") escape—a conversion experience, a repentant prayer, or a confessional moment—are clearly more about anxiety and fear of death *within the concerned person* than they are about God's presence and its relationship to salvation.

A *genuine* concern for the dying's heavenly assurance necessarily begins with embracing them in their suffering and affirming the truth of the immediate presence of the Divine.

There's a type of false freedom that is manufactured during the holidays, an implicit promise that we can experience freedom from the grief and struggle that make up most of our "non-holiday" lives if we participate in the holiday cheer, the festivities, and the merriment. If we buy into the holiday experience—both emotionally and financially—pain can be averted. There's a salvation promise in the holidays bought into at every store bedecked with inventory to create the exact holiday experience each of us needs.

Dad was being crucified this Christmas, and no amount of manufacturing could produce the type of holiday cheer necessary to escape the suffering. There was nothing merry about it. We were effectively stricken with two wounds: the wound of losing the pseudo-freedom promised during the holidays *and* Dad's crucifixion notice.

Dad's diagnosis was a Christmas present from hell, a forever reminder of his death sentence. On Christmas Eve, after the presents were wrapped, the stockings were stuffed, and my whole family was peacefully asleep, a war still raged in my mind. On one side was the belief that Dad needed religious certainty, belief in heaven, and salvation. On the other side was a desire to simply name the suffering and embrace my father.

I wrote Mom and Dad a letter late that night. Part of it read:

> This Christmas Eve is different. I'm crying. I've kissed each of my kids good night. In their eyes I saw hope and excitement. But there's a heaviness in me, a heart weighted by the burden of bad news. The cookies are on the counter and the music of old hymns are filling the living room, but my heart hurts. Mom and Dad, I know your hearts hurt too.

Christmas marks the event of the incarnation in the midst of a world full of pain; Jesus was born into the unpleasant texture of this life. That sure sounds lovely, but *that* Christmas Eve, in the middle of writing to my parents, more questions demanded my attention.

Could Christmas really offer a solution to pervasive pain? Could it at least smooth out the rough edges of suffering? Would Dad experience any freedom?

There's a difference between the freedom promised by the Christmas holiday—the one we were missing by not joining in the festivities—and the freedom promised by the incarnation of Christmas. The former is freedom *from* suffering by distancing oneself from it with eggnog and tinsel and pictures with Santa; the latter is a freedom *within* suffering by way of embracing it. The former is temporary and relies on distraction, while the latter is real, fleshly, and lasting.

Christmas suggests that freedom from suffering is not a temporary distraction from it but the tangible experience of fearless love in the face of it. True freedom—that which we might call "Divine freedom" since it's incarnational—is experienced in *how* we love during suffering, not *what* we purport as a solution for suffering.

In Philippians 3:10, Paul wanted to share in Christ's suffering because it is in the sharing of pain that we experience the deepest freedom from the isolation and meaninglessness of suffering alone. Together, in this world, in these bodies that experience pain and suffering, there is the possibility of freedom from hell.

My letter to Mom and Dad continued with what I was learning about Christmas:

> Sometimes when we're hurting, grieving, and suffering we feel alone. You're not alone, Mom and Dad. I'm here with you. I'm crying with you. I'm writing through tears this Christmas Eve with you. This moment in this darkness, we are together. Perhaps that's the good news . . . we're not alone. Darkness lasts forever only to the lonely, the isolated. And we're not alone.

Words on a page may sound nice, but they need flesh (John 1:14). I tried to express that even though we were not joining in the holiday cheer, there was a deeper, more lasting freedom that could be experienced in the very embracing of the truth of

Christmas. I wanted to physically be with Dad; I needed to be with Dad. Would being together in suffering allow us both to be free to feel and cry and be fully ourselves?

Would we experience a sense of freedom from the torture of ALS?

Would we touch heaven by embracing the suffering of Dad's crucifixion?

Soon we would find out.

I was compelled to buy myself a Christmas present: a round-trip ticket to California to visit my father. I could no longer theorize about Christmas and incarnation; I needed to test them out. I needed to embody the belief that heaven can be found in the here-and-now, in the flesh, even in suffering.

I woke up Christmas morning thinking about my father. The rest of the family was still sleeping, so I sat at the dining room table overlooking the snow-banked Moyie River and reflected on real, fleshly, heart-felt love.

For years I understood my disconnection from Dad to be a type of confinement, like a reptile in an aquarium behind clear glass. Though my environment was rather pleasant as a boy, I was close and yet profoundly distant from my father. There was a clear partition between us through which his love couldn't penetrate.

I envied my childhood friend's relationship with his father. Josh's father provided an "affirming" type of love. Sometimes it was a wink and a finger point before he left for work. Other times it was a compliment about Josh's basketball shot or his latest success at our favorite fishing hole. Josh's father always seemed to be telling him, "You matter, you are a success, and your peculiar interests are important to me."

I wanted love the way Josh received it, in the form of compliments and affirmation. There was love, but the loving connection I longed for was absent because the specific type of love I was looking for didn't exist. As an adult I've learned that the glass is not so much a glass entrapment imposed from without, but it was instead a filter that I've created out of my own ignorance, which itself is a type of entrapment imposed from within. As I said earlier, the type of love I was *expecting* was simply not there.

After a Little League game, for example, I'd hop into Dad's small Toyota pickup, hungry to hear, "Good game, bud," or, "Great playing out there." That's not what I received. Instead, my father would list a dozen ways I could improve batting and base running. I was always left hungry.

I wonder if Dad was imprisoned by his expectations, his ignorance. Was he waiting for a son's love that looked and felt and was shaped a certain way? Was he trapped behind a glass wall that was an inherited expectation from his own father? Was he enslaved by the absence of a particular kind of son's responsive love that differed from the one I was giving?

Love is never the perfect fulfillment of what one wants it to be. It never meets expectations. In a sense, if it did, it would cease to be love at all. Love is always partially unpredictable because it is fully contingent on the freedom of its giver and therefore a surprise to the recipient.

This is why love is not necessarily a thing, an object to be given and received, predefined and expected. Love is that which names the surprise itself. Love is not exchanged; love names the event whereby two people are open to being loved on each other's terms. This is why love is hard work, not because loving someone is necessarily a chore (though it may be), but because it is difficult to cultivate the ability—against years of formed expectations—to experience love that is unfamiliar. We are all ignorant to love at first, and it's something that must be learned to be received.

Ignorance is a precondition for love, I think. Love doesn't demand ignorance; rather, being aware of and accepting my own ignorance creates in me the disposition to receive the surprise that is love. Practically speaking, owning the glass entrapment of my own expectations—accepting my own limiting expectations of and attempts to control love—was an important ingredient in receiving the surprising love of Dad.

My limitation in understanding the diverse ways by which a father can love a son was at once the cause of my blindness to love *and* a condition for receiving it. It seemed for so long to be a curse of bondage, but now I was beginning to recognize it as a blessed limitation. Inarguably, it was always prophetic. My ignorance was a foretelling of the love I was becoming open to in my upcoming visit with my Father as he approached death.

The Hebrews were waiting for a new Moses to liberate them from under the oppressive thumb of Roman rule. They were waiting for a new David to build up an army and overpower the might of the Empire. Liberation came, but it came by a surprisingly more powerful means than expected. It came by way of love and peaceableness.

Israel was blind to the means by which liberation would come. Like me, they were ignorant. But Israel's ignorance was a precondition to receive life-altering Divine love. We might say that John the Baptizer's primary role was to expose ignorance, as that is a fundamental first step in experiencing the magnitude of the coming liberation manifested through the embodiment of the Divine love in Jesus Christ.

I was waiting for many years for a type of liberation out of my reptilian confinement—a breakthrough in my relationship with Dad. Israel wanted out from under Rome's rule, and I wanted into Dad's love. In both cases there was ignorance needing to be exposed. And in both cases a mangled body would bear witness to that love and liberation.

One would hang on a cross.

One would lay emaciated in a bed.

II

HOPE LOST

*We had hoped he was
the one who was going
to redeem Israel.*

— LUKE 24:21

5

LEGACY

I ARRIVED AT DAD'S HOUSE ON THURSDAY, JANUARY SIXTH. IT HAD been less than two weeks since my father's official diagnosis, but Mom had said she could see the symptoms for over a year. That was how long it had been since I saw my father last, and his physical appearance showed every bit of a year of wrangling with a deadly disease.

Dad's steel blue eyes remained, but every other physical trait was drained of vitality. His hair was disheveled and thin. His protruding cheekbones, slender neck, and boney shoulders looked borrowed from a man thirty years his elder. Even his hands, once strong and commanding, were frail.

I'll never forget the moment I opened the front door and saw my father sitting in his blue leather chair in the corner of the living room. I kicked off my shoes and walked briskly toward him, trying to swallow the panic that was creeping into my throat. I wasn't prepared for his frailty. He seemed half the size he was a year before. I leaned in and gave him a gentle hug.

When I pulled back, he wore a big smile, and some of my nerves calmed.

I sat on the couch and grabbed the first framed picture I saw on the end table between his chair and the couch I sat on. It was his father and mother, whom we called Nonno and Nonna. We sat quietly for a moment as I studied the picture.

"Tell me about Nonno and Nonna, Dad."

"My father was the hardest worker I'd ever met," he said. Dad went on to tell me stories about the disparity of Nonno's small stature and his strength. He reflected specifically about the time when my grandfather lined the driveway of my childhood home with boulders that he moved entirely by hand. And of his mother he said, "She was faithful to her Catholic beliefs until the day she died. I always respected that."

Nonno and Nonna left quite a legacy for my father. He inherited their substantial work ethic and piety, though they took on different forms, as legacies often do from generation to generation.

Dad also inherited his parents' stamina. He was an educator. Stamina in the field of education looks quite different from digging ditches, chopping firewood, and pruning hedges, but it takes its own toll on the body. For Dad, being the "hardest worker" in the spirit of Nonno meant exceeding every expectation placed on him. He was the first to school in the morning and the last to leave in the afternoon. One week before summer's end, he would prepare and organize his classroom for his students. When school would let out for vacation, Dad would tweak lessons, sort files, and organize desks (his own and the students') until the campus was vacant. Dad was the hardest working teacher I'd ever met.

Dad appreciated Nonna's piety, as she privately prayed and attended Mass her entire life. While Mom, all four of my brothers, and I were all drawn to Christianity, my father was not compelled by religion. He translated Nonna's fidelity to God into a loyalty and commitment to mastering his teaching subject. For most of his career, Dad taught junior high social studies. He approached his work ethic as if pursuing tenure at a university. To this day, my father was the only person I know who could answer most questions on *Jeopardy*. It was the result of studying history, the result of fidelity to the task of becoming an excellent teacher.

Dad believed in doing a job with excellence and doing it over the course of many years. It was the Fasani legacy. And that's what he did, every day, for over three decades.

It was only natural that he would do the same when it came to recovery. For a whole year before he was officially diagnosed with ALS, Dad lost nearly sixty pounds, struggled with breathing, and eventually lost the ability to walk without assistance. But he hadn't lost hope. He applied the Fasani legacy of hard work and fidelity to reversing his weakness. With Nonno's stamina in his heart and Nonna's unwavering fidelity in his bones, Dad waged a noble fight against his mysterious ailment. His body severely atrophied and dependent on a walker, he still stubbornly and faithfully shuffled laps around the property, hoping for strength to return to his muscles and an appetite to his stomach.

He finally received those atrocious three letters from the doctor: ALS. Receiving that diagnosis is like a ticking box in the mail with an affixed note that says, "Bomb inside." The amount of time remaining is a mystery, but the outcome is certain. After receiving the bomb of a diagnosis, it was only a matter of time until the inevitable detonation of life.

I was only one hour into my visit and I was surprised by the complexity of my father's disease. Only thirteen days before my visit, death became more real. The diagnosis meant that there was no possibility of recovery. But something more profound, more deeply nestled in the enclaves of Dad's identity died too: the efficacy of the Fasani legacy. No amount of hard work and commitment to mastery influenced the inevitable. While the legacy lived on in memory, death set in and there was no turning back.

THE TWO DISCIPLES—CLEOPAS and his brother (who is unnamed) —on the road to Emmaus were Jewish men reared in the hope of God's freeing intervention. They bounced on their grandfather's lap as children and heard stories of daring prophets that redirected their ancestors toward faithfulness. They sat around campfires, listening intently to their father tell stories of God's liberation and faithful patriarchs that risked lives for freedom and righteousness. The wager of their lives was not a rash decision nor a diluted impulse. The brothers found themselves providentially participating in the very liberating story of God.

And then Jesus was crucified. He lost.

Walking from Jerusalem to Emmaus was not only a walk of disappointment, but it was also a walk replete with confusion and doubt. The very meaning of their lives and the coherence of their beliefs were at stake. In following Jesus, they wagered their lives, but the reward was guaranteed! It was an investment into a people, a history, a reality that included their participation. Their investment returned void, empty, dead. Their memories persisted, but in practice, the messianic movement was futile. We could say that a legacy of hope—one marked by liberation of a people, of a land, of a way of life—was dead.

But like the men on that walk of death to Emmaus, something profoundly changed in Dad. The inevitable reality of death set in for Dad and for the disciples. In sharp contrast, and almost paradoxically, a glimmer of freedom also set in. As if in the trauma of the diagnostic ALS bomb, a burden was shaken loose. A bit of freedom inhabited his soul.

There is a general cultural norm that separates men from emotions. Feelings can only be expressed under specified arrangements, usually in private, often not at all. Dad believed emotions were a private matter. For years, he swallowed his feelings of fear, depression, and insecurity, and he repressed his feelings of intimacy and affection.

However, traumatic loss and grief challenge the cultural norms. There is often an emotional flexibility, as if the soul takes liberty to free the ego from following the rules. While the burden of Dad's inevitable death and the humility of being dependent on Mom were a type of confinement, Dad experienced some freedom. He was freed to feel. He was freed to lament and cry. And most profoundly, he was experiencing a freedom to talk about those feelings. I wondered, *Is the possibility of a new legacy emerging from the rubble of death?* The freedom Dad was experiencing was a small but profound freedom.

I imagine the two brothers experienced a similar freedom on their walk back home. As they walked back to Emmaus, they grieved. They exchanged regrets and fears, condolences and apologies. They were emotionally unstable but in a mutual show of support, "They were talking with each other about everything" (v14). For the first time, in a type of unsaid pact that occurs after shared trauma, they abandoned their emotional stoicism and wept together publicly. And without reservation, they talked about all that had happened.

My father was also on that walk.

6

DEPRESSION

When I was young, in the eighties and nineties, I always remember my Dad being stressed. Every noise was too loud, every laughter too rambunctious. The burden manifested in a perpetual somberness and quick temper. When my father wasn't at work, his demeanor and stress made for a volatile home environment.

As I got older, I made a few discoveries in the most unlikely way. Two years before my father's diagnosis, I was living and pastoring on the Big Island of Hawaii. I was exhausted from being overworked and meeting with a therapist once a week. I struggled with bouts of darkness and depression, and in order to better understand these challenges, my therapist encouraged me to exchange letters with my parents. Mom was intrigued and committed to being my pen pal.

My mother and I explored our family history, our unique family system, and some of the thinking that went into her parenting style. The letters became a type of extended genogram, exploring the relational connections between people, events, and behaviors in the Fasani and Merrill (her maiden name) families. The letter writing was enriching and insightful. As I'm sure my therapist knew, the letters were a slow and thoughtful way to build trust, lubricating discussion about long-avoided hardships.

One surprising discovery from those letters was the nature of my father's stress. As far back as Mom could remember, Dad suffered from a fear of losing control of the simple things, like missing an appointment or forgetting to mail a letter. Two extremes bore down on him continually: he was wrenched with the stress of everyday mishaps, and he was exhausted from being so tightly wound. My father struggled with a type of anxious lethargy.

There was another discovery I made through those letters. My father's struggles were unmanageable. Most adults wrestle with having a bad day or a lack of motivation at work. Those sensations are manageable. He was stricken with something much deeper, more overwhelming.

After months of exchanging letters, Mom finally painted a verbal picture with haunting vividness. In one of her letters, she wrote: "He used to lay on the floor of our bedroom with the lights off and his hands folded across his chest. He would just lay there and moan. You boys would be downstairs."

My impatience got the better of me while I read those lines. I picked up the phone and called her. "Mom, I just read your letter. How often did Dad lay on the floor with the lights off? Once, twice maybe?"

"No, many times," she said. "There were stretches of time when he simply couldn't cope, couldn't do *anything* but lay there with arms folded, eyes closed, next to his bed."

"Mom, that should have been treated," I barked.

"I know," she said.

I needed to say it out loud for myself more than for my mother. She already knew. Whether she had the language to properly name it at the time didn't matter at that point. I needed to give it a name, to put it out there, to publicly display what my father hid for so long. "Mom! Dad was not only stressed, he was severely depressed. Severely depressed! He needed medication!"

Unfortunately, in my immediate family, but also my extended family, depression is stigmatized. I remember with clarity the conversations we had at family gatherings about mental illness. When the topic turned toward depression, not only did we debate its cause, we debated whether the psychological phenomenon even existed. I learned early on that using the word is asking for a certain amount of judgment.

I wanted to talk to Dad about depression, but I knew I had to approach the topic at an angle, not head-on. I coached myself: *Don't talk about depression. Talk about Dad being overwhelmed. Don't use the word* depression. *Talk about the years when his body wouldn't allow him to perform basic tasks. Not depression.*

I was so worked up about my strategy that my lower back started tightening, which is an early sign of anxiety. The self-coaching was making me panic.

From my seat on the couch, I could look through the window at the hills I used to explore as a boy. I remember dressing in army fatigues and hiking boots for my hunting expeditions. BB gun in hand, I combed the hills and open pastures behind our house looking for rabbits and squirrels. It didn't matter if I saw any critters, let alone shoot anything. Anyone who's been "hunting" with a child knows that the prey is not the point of the hunt— the hunt itself is the point. The dressing up, the tracking, the exploration.

I was putting the emphasis on the wrong target, which was contributing to my anxiety. The target was not the word or the concept or even the experience of depression. The target was to meaningfully and truthfully connect with Dad, bearing in mind a fuller understanding of his emotional landscape. The value is in the exploration, the journey along the way. I reminded myself: *It's not about* the depression. *It's about the discovery, the journey, the connection. It's about the uncharted territory of our common history. Invite him to explore.*

Since his diagnosis, Dad had already shown infinitely more emotional flexibility—freedom to feel and share feelings. So on that Thursday, I invited Dad to explore. "Tell me about when I was young. Was life tough back then?" I asked.

I'll never know if Dad would have resisted a question about depression. I don't even know if my entry point was at the right angle. What I do know is that something went correctly. What followed was an hour-long conversation about a five-year period of emotional treachery. I can't possibly capture all that Dad said, but it was moving and eye-opening. In terms of connecting with and understanding Dad, it was nothing short of revelatory. More importantly, it was freeing for him to name and share his experience of an otherwise taboo topic.

According to my father, 1978 through 1983 were the "five years of hell." Rick and Rob were young and needy. Randy was born in 1978, I was born in 1980, and Rocky was born in 1982. Five young boys. That alone is enough to cause serious bouts of stress. But that wasn't all.

While Mom was pregnant with Randy, my parents worked on building a house in Roseville, California, while they lived in Sacramento. Two weeks before Randy was born, Nonna died. Shortly after completing the house, I was born, and shortly after that, we moved to Porterville, California. Between Sacramento and Porterville, Dad changed careers from teaching to real estate. And then Rocky came along. We moved back to Roseville permanently, and Dad went back to teaching.

Three children, three moves, two career changes, one house built, and one death all in five years.

"Those five years felt like five years of hell," Dad said abruptly.

"Did you have any outlets?"

"Back then, you didn't talk about it," he quickly replied.

"It comes out in other ways, right?" I asked, though the question implied my personal belief.

After a long pause, he explained, "It was tough. I was angry. I was *depressed.* No outlets. Back then you didn't talk or share those kinds of things. I swallowed it and moved on." He looked off in the distance as if his memory was taking him back to that time.

It was quiet. The silence was heavy.

The stigma that forced Dad to swallow that experience, those feelings, that oppressive sense of darkness, was losing control. He named it. He named the depression from hell, which is the first enormous step toward emotional liberty.

It was still quiet.

I waited, not showing that internally I sensed a tremendous amount of release. I didn't want to assert, or even suggest, an agenda. *Would he take a step further, freeing himself even more of that confinement? Would he add any detail, releasing himself even further from the years of repressing those feelings?*

He said with some hesitation, "I would lay in my closet sometimes and just keep it in." He paused to gather his thoughts, as if every step forward was a calculated negotiation. "I would lay there in the dark. I had a family to take care of, bills to pay. I was trying to control the depression." He looked at the blank wall. "It was too much, Ryan. I had too much to take care of and just couldn't handle it."

I was taken to that place Mom described as "next to his bed" and my dad described as "in the closet." Dad was severely depressed during those years, incapacitated at times, and life was not distributing any slack.

Moving, babies, death, building houses . . . these are the classic life transitions. We have the emotional capacity to handle them, but maybe only one or two at a time. Dad and Mom bore them all. My father and I explored his "five years of hell," and *it* was finally named. We looked at depression in the eyes and weakened it of its two greatest strengths: hiding and silence.

ANGER

First-century Palestine was an honor-shame society, which is a helpful context to understand the failure Cleopas and his brother were bearing as they returned home after the crucifixion. Honor is closely associated to one's social status because honor is the approval mechanism used to affirm behaviors that align with social expectations. Those expectations are a claim to social value that is recognized by a particular social group.

In this way, honor does more than influence one's public reputation; instead, honor *is* one's reputation. Even further, because honor is so closely associated to inclusion into a particular social group (when behavior aligns with expectations), social value and self-worth become conflated. The experience of exclusion to effectively have zero positive value to a particular group—is the quintessence of worthlessness.

Shame, for Cleopas and his brother, is the lack of honor. Honor is approval and affirmation, inclusion, and personal value.

Shame is disapproval and humiliation, exclusion, and worthlessness. They knew that following Jesus, who undermined the value of social status (see Luke 14), posed a threat to their continued acceptance in their social group, their community. They were quite certain that if the Jesus movement failed, their lives might be forever marked by public shame and exclusion. Their walk home was literally a walk of shame, a stroll toward possible worthlessness.

Shame begins as behavioral control, but it doesn't end there. It conveys the message that one's worth is diminished as the result of behavior. In other words, shame cuts to the core of one's inherent value by using behavior as an entry point. But shame is a double-edged sword. The first cut is the initial shaming by others, and the second cut is the self-criticism that births out of the experience. When a condition is unavoidable, shame thrives, for behavior that can't be averted is inevitably associated with self-worth. This is why shame is a double abuse: the shaming by others serves as training ground for self-shame. Eventually, the victim turns the sword in on himself and inflicts his own wounds.

As my father and I talked, I realized how much shame he felt. "If I had said anything about being depressed, I would have never heard the end of it from my own father. I knew I shouldn't have been depressed. I needed to just push through," he said.

"What does your dad have to do with your depression as an adult?" I asked, aware that at some level we are always children trying to please (and compete with) our fathers.

"Nonno never had a bad day. I couldn't either."

"Did he say that, or was it implied?"

"I just knew it. Never talked about. It was just known." He nodded between each statement, as if he was convincing himself of each.

"So, you were depressed but had to hide it? That itself is depressing."

"Oh yeah. I was stuck. I just couldn't do it. I couldn't say anything." Shaking his head, he said regretfully, "I shouldn't have been depressed, but we made it, didn't we?"

As we talked, I got a glimpse of Dad's childhood shame. He, like so many boys and young men, was shamed for his feelings. The shame was internalized, which was why it didn't need to be discussed. As an adult, Dad "just knew" he wasn't allowed to have a bad day. He was stuck in his own silence and shame. The sword was turned inward and self-criticism became habitual. An internal battle raged inside of him. He believed the awful lie that feelings are wrong, and though natural, must be suppressed.

In adulthood, Dad didn't allow himself to feel depressed. He tried to hide the fact that the darkness was overwhelming, telling himself that his feelings were failures. He suffered a life of self-inflicted wounds. His own self-criticism attempted to balance his own shaming. He felt the full weight of worthlessness and exclusion. The disciples feared shame upon their return, which was fundamentally the same fear my father had: worthlessness and exclusion.

But not all of our conversation was intense and heavy. I talked about how beautiful Idaho is in the winter, I described some of the improvements we made on the property, and I updated him on my kids. Dad seemed to enjoy the break from talking about shame, but the weight of the room seemed to lean toward sensitive topics.

My father cut in at one point and said, "I'm so mad. I'm so angry I'll miss everything."

I realized I was sharing about the present, but I was inadvertently sharing about what my father would miss out on in the future. It made me realize that he wasn't *only* angry about what he'd miss tomorrow or the next day; he was angry about the past.

"I've missed so much already. I've been angry for so long, it seems."

What was this anger? Was it directed at something or someone? Did he mean another word? Strangely, I found my answers while discussing sports.

My father was a huge sports fan. Sacramento was only thirty minutes from my childhood home. San Francisco was two hours. That meant the Kings, the 49ers, and the Giants were our home teams. Dad had the uncanny ability to keep track of all the stats on all three teams at all times. I can still hear my father's grumbling when he disagreed with a referee's call, which was usually a call against one of *our* teams.

My father was a formidable athlete himself. He lettered in three sports in high school and was regularly acknowledged as a star in his local paper's Sports page.

"I know you loved sports, Dad. Who taught you to play so well? Was it Nonno?"

"No, my dad wasn't much of an athlete."

"What does 'much of an athlete' mean?"

"My dad was the most coordinated person I ever knew. He could leap between rocks, keep his balance under any circumstance. Really, really athletic. Incredibly strong. But he knew nothing about sports. He was just an immigrant kid. Back then, immigrant kids worked more than they played."

"Did Uncle Rick teach you?" I asked. My father was one of three children. The oldest, Shirley, was five years older than my father, and Rick was three years older than Dad. I knew a lot about Aunt Shirley, and we saw her occasionally for holidays and family get-togethers. She's artistic and generous and wonderful. And she always had an excess of compliments for me growing up. I knew very little about my uncle Rick, but I do remember my father having admiration for his athleticism.

"My brother had to teach himself everything, but it didn't take long. He learned quickly because he was such a natural athlete," he said.

"Did Rick teach you?"

"Yeah . . ." he said but with some doubt in his voice. "But Rick gravitated toward individual sports in high school. He was very athletic."

"You were a team sport guy, right?" I was fishing for how my Nonno, Uncle Rick, and my father's athleticism might fit together.

"Yes, I was more into team sports," he answered. "You know the neat thing about Rick. When we were younger, he let me play with all of his friends. I was much younger. No one else's little brother played with Rick's friends, but he made sure I was there. That's how I got good."

I thought of my relationships with my own brothers. Rick and Rob were too old to include me in their pick-up basketball games in the front yard. But on occasion, Randy would ask me to play with he and his friends. Outsized, I tried my hardest to not get trampled. Occassionally I'd contribute, but mostly I just took up space. I treasured those opportunities and believe it's because he inlcuded me that I have so much respect for him today.

"We were close. I looked up to him so much." Nostalgia in his voice, he said, "My parents just loved Rick." Then in a moment stacked with layers of meaning and emotion, Dad said, "And he was taken from them by that drunk driver. They never let go. They were so angry, especially my mom."

I was reticent to dive into deeper emotional waters, but I had so many questions. "Did they go to the grave with that anger?" I asked.

He grimaced. "I think so."

The sheer permanence of that thought—dying with unresolved anger—brought the conversation to a halt. We sat quietly for a long moment. Dad wore a vestige of the grimace on his face. I stared at my feet, surprised my question about sports ended with death.

There seemed to be a thread that tied together Dad's memory of Rick's inclusion of him as a younger brother, his parents' love for Rick and traumatic loss, and the resentment his parents harbored for the rest of their lives.

Brother's love. Parents' love. Death. Anger. What held them together?

Dad treasured his relationship with his brother, who affirmed him as a boy, gave him the tools to assimilate into adolescent culture, brought him under his wing, and in a way gave him wings to fly on his own. I realized in that conversation that Rick was a type of father figure for Dad, a conduit to adulthood in all matters of importance for a young man. Rick was to thank for that. And then he was gone.

Psychological projection is a concept that suggests we project onto others that which is unpleasant within us. It's a defense mechanism to avoid conscious conflict and anxiety. We attribute to someone else the thoughts, feelings, impulses, or desires that we cannot accept and deal with. While those very thoughts and impulses may be present in the other, we will exaggerate them to justify putting off our own thoughts or impulses.

The grimace on Dad's face when he acknowledged that his parents died with harbored anger was a projection of his own feelings—a fear that he would go to his own grave embroiled in anger. The very thought of dying with unresolved anger was overwhelming. It reflected back to him an imminent threat that he may suffer the same fate.

We were quiet after that for a long while. No doubt my father's mind was swirling with memories. It was the first time he'd discussed his brother Rick in such detail. When my father was eighteen, Rick was in a fatal car accident. My father was stricken with anger since that day.

"How did you manage after your brother's death?" I asked, breaking the silence.

"I don't know, Ryan . . . I don't know."

Unapologetically, I said, "I'd walk right into a church and tell God how I felt, even if that required a middle finger. I couldn't hold on to that weight." I was even shocked by my reaction, but I got caught up in the moment.

With a slight grin, Dad said, "Oh, I did . . . and I still do occasionally."

"Well, at least you're talking to God in some way. It's better than holding it in."

"I've been talking to God a lot more lately," he quickly responded.

Gratitude and sorrow wrestled within me, competing for my attention. Part of me was satisfied knowing Dad was talking through his anger with God. I chose to think of it as a type of fist-shaking prayer. Another part of me, however, was mourning the fact that he had harbored anger for so long. Rick's tragic death stalked Dad, preying on his very sanity for fifty years! And now, years later, my father was finally talking about it.

Talking can be the salt for the slug of anger that consumes the vitality of one's heart. Talking, like salt, is painful on wounds, but it shrivels up anger over time. It dries up anger's strength, steals its life. I hoped that talking to God about his anger, as well as talking to me, might serve this purpose for Dad.

Talking and anger. Fist-shaking prayer and tragedy.

I imagine the disciples on the road to Emmaus were talking as a way of coping with anger. I imagine they were doing a fair share of fist-shaking prayer and grimacing at the very thought of their loss. I imagine Dad, then, is in good company.

8

HONESTY

I'VE HEARD STORY AFTER STORY ABOUT SELF-TRAINED EVANGELISTS converting non-believers on their deathbed. There is an urgency to deliver the Good News to the dying because salvation is at stake.

Good intentions? Yes. Healthy? For Dad, no.

Our Thursday conversation made that clear. I asked him if religious concerns became more prominent with the onset of terminal illness. He confirmed they did. I asked gently, "Are you leaning on your Catholic upbringing to wade through some of the concerns?"

My father was brought up culturally Catholic. It wasn't practiced in his home, but they attended Mass during the holidays. It was fire insurance, in a way—just enough church to avoid hell.

Nonna, my father's mom, was the most pious in their family, and she went to Mass and prayed often. Nonno, my father's dad, wasn't religious at all, but attended when pushed. This was similar to the religious dynamic in our home growing up.

My mother was a religious seeker. We tried small churches and big churches. We dabbled in Mormonism and fundamental Christianity. When Mom finally "gave her life to the Lord," all the religious seeking stopped. All she wanted was a place that "preached the Word of God," and we found it in a Baptist church with a sizable children's department and multiple worship service options. Every Sunday, my mother would load the five of us boys—our shirts tucked in, socks pulled high, and hair perfectly parted on the left side—into the station wagon and we headed off to church.

Dad never came along. If pressed, he'd say he was religiously neutral.

"My mother was pretty private, so she never talked about her faith. But we often saw her praying. And she always went to Mass. I always respected her for that," Dad said.

I picked up the double message: Dad respected that his mother practiced her faith and that she practiced it privately. And I understood why he never said anything to me about my choice to continue practicing Christianity into adulthood and eventually enter the ministry. So long as it stayed private, he was supportive.

With this in mind, I confessed, "I might be asking you religious questions because I know we're both interested in ultimate meaning, but I promise I'm not gonna pressure you with my beliefs."

"Good to know. Good to know." He paused and had a pensive look on his face. "Then maybe you can explain why Christians are so pushy."

I knew immediately that my commitment to not pressure Dad with my beliefs was going to be harder to uphold than I initially thought. I didn't have an agenda, but the role reversal caught me by surprise. *Could I answer without sounding defensive? Could I be honest and not pushy? Was I going to be able to keep my promise?*

The church Mom found when we were young espoused the central doctrine of evangelicalism, namely, salvation comes through the atoning sacrifice of Jesus Christ. Our pastors preached from the Bible, which usually meant an hour of storytelling interlaced with verses from the New Testament.

Every Sunday, I heard a different version of the same salvation story: Everyone is guilty of sin and forbidden from heaven, but through the death of Jesus sins are forgiven and heavenly entrance admitted. It's formulaic, it's simple, it's attractive. For many it offers solace, rounding off the sharp edges of our inevitable death. If one can be certain to go to heaven, then the very thought of death becomes more bearable. One doesn't have to die at all but instead lives forever. *What joy must come from the belief that one can eternally live?* (That's the exact rhetorical question I remember hearing from the pulpit.)

Closely related to the formula for salvation was the case for proselytizing. Proselytizing is simply the overflow of the joy from being saved. The syllogism went something like this: salvation is simple; salvation is abundantly joyful; joy is therefore simple. So, what is simple can be shared simply. Proselytizing is as easy as sharing how simply people can experience a life of joy. "It should just spill out of us, right onto others," I remember one of my youth leaders saying.

But when I was in sixth grade, while wandering around the church campus one day after being kicked out of Sunday School class, I became less convinced. I wondered where this so-called joy was. My Sunday School teachers didn't seem full of joy. My family, especially Mom and Dad's relationship, always seemed on edge. And here I was at church not feeling particularly joyful.

I wondered: *If joy is so simple, and evangelism oozes out of the saved, then why is our house and church full of strife?* I would also wonder specifically about Dad who was not "saved" and Mom who "knew the Lord." *Why is Dad not saved yet if it's so simple? Why is he not at church if this is where joy is found with such ease? And why is Mom always yelling?*

Truth be told, what a twelve-year-old can poke holes in is probably not made of theological Kevlar. That's because religious formation is more organic, less manufactured. I've always understood it more like a taproot that penetrates my psychological and emotional makeup, unwilling to be yanked out. So questioning the logic of an unhealthy understanding of salvation (or joy, or evangelism) isn't a threat. Taproots go deep and aren't easily uprooted.

Since the sixth grade I've asked hard questions (evidently, some challenging enough to earn me expulsion from Sunday School), and still remnants of those religious roots remain deep within me. So deep that I forgot they existed until Dad's question exposed them.

I said, "The formula is simple; the reward is huge. Christians get excited about how easy it is to go to heaven, and in their zeal, they sorta push it on people."

Instead of answering why evangelicals are so pushy (Dad's negative experience), I focused on why they are so excited and zealous (my positive spin). My impulse was to defend the formula and by extension the pushiness. Like a sibling who compulsively defends against a bully, I felt a biological affinity to the bad theology, the formulaic syllogisms, the platitudes, and needed to protect them. They weren't correct, but they were deep within me.

"That simple, huh?" Dad responded. But the look he gave me said more. He blinked hard, as if to add that not all simple solutions to finitude are good answers, nor do they excuse overbearing pushiness. He was correct, and I knew it.

I said to myself several times before it sunk in: *Tell him the damn truth, already.*

I gained my courage and went at it again without the positive spin. (Yes, I did feel like I was betraying my former pastor and every Sunday School teacher I had until high school.)

I gulped down the apprehension. "I think evangelicals are pushy because . . . well, they're sincere about what they believe but insecure about the credibility of it. They are really excited about the salvation formula, but they—"

I paused for a moment to negotiate the consequence of externalizing my explanation. If I used the pronoun "they," I was not implicated in the embarrassing pushiness of many evangelicals. Dad was asking *me*, as an authority, as one who ought to know. He was asking about *my* Christian identity and the religious roots that tapped deep into who *I* was.

I needed to own who I was, but to avoid it—even subtly, even gracefully—would be dishonest. To own it meant I needed to look the salvation formula in the eye and name it for what it was. As much as I disliked the association with the Christians to which Dad was referring, I was indeed one of them, at least in name.

I continued with a little more confidence. "*We . . .* are not honest about *our* doubts and uncertainties. *Our* formulas don't even match *our* experience. *We're* insecure. And that comes out in pushiness, even aggression . . . and an overuse of platitudes. They're defense mechanisms of sorts."

There was a gentle satisfaction that followed. Dad knew my answer was more honest, more direct, more *me*. His eyes told me that he was interested in hearing more.

"But when our simple formulas are challenged—if they don't line up with experience or reason—we cope with classic defense mechanisms. We push. We criticize. We scapegoat. It's easier to recycle and defend what's familiar than to admit uncertainty," I said.

Admittedly inarticulate, Dad connected with what I was saying. "I really appreciate that, Ryan. I personally enjoy parts of Christianity, the tradition and history mostly, but I don't like the dishonest pushiness." He shook his head and rolled out a soft grunt, another testament to his dislike for assertive proselytizing.

I nodded. I'm sure it appeared that I was merely nodding in agreement—and I was in part—but I was also nodding in delight at the connection we'd made over an explicitly religious subject matter. Despite the fact that I have studied religion for the entirety of my adult life and Dad was a history buff with a knowledge base of world religions across time, he and I connected in a meaningful way about religion for the first time. We sat quietly as we shared our unspoken gratitude for this new bond.

After some time, Dad broke the silence. "I mostly do church by myself. Watch Mass every so often. And I talk to God . . . and Shirley."

There are nearly fifty evangelical Christians in my father's immediate and extended family who are devout, biblically literate, and zealous to share their understanding of truth. But when it comes to conversations about church and religion, Dad chose to talk to his sister Shirley. She doesn't qualify as any of the aforementioncd. Aunt Shirley is sensitive to religious diversity, but more importantly (or, perhaps consequently), she doesn't need to defend religious formula or feel the need to offer religious platitudes. Dad was repulsed by pushy clichés. He wanted honesty, which was why he'd call Shirley. Now, in the face of the ultimate future, he wanted honesty and presence.

The simple answers that are pressured onto the dying are not at all indicative of certainty but of insecurity. I was learning that platitudinous theology is often the result of a deep need to know in the face of the unknown. The inevitable uncertainty we all experience is met with a type of fabricated knowing where provisional beliefs become permanent facts. But the facts are built on a foundation full of repressed questions, ignored doubts, denied uncertainty.

The very nature of death—unpredictable, uncontrollable— challenges formulas and facts. It reminds us of how little control we truly have, so we push back and assert our answers as a means of coping with (or defending against) the uncertainty of death.

The content of our conversation was not the only thing that was religious. Our connection—our honesty together, our presence together—became sacred. I began the conversation with a question about religious concerns becoming more prominent in the face of death. In a way the question took a back seat to the experience, which was an answer in itself: religious concerns don't increase in the face of death as much as the need for the experience of sacred connection.

I finally, and for the first time with Dad, owned my uncertainty. I learned that what emerges when platitudes and pushiness are set aside is the possibility of a sacred bond. I was confessional about the formulas and the overbearing proselytizing, which was a definitive loss of hope in the unhealthy evangelical roots still deeply imbedded within me.

However, in the midst of lost hope for both me and Dad—the dark and dreary road of lost dreams, lost strength, lost faith, and the imminent loss of life—we deeply connected. We connected through affirming, not challenging, his religious sentiments. We connected through patient conversation and long moments of silence. We connected because I was honest, even confessional, not knowing and not pretending to know.

We connected because I was present. I didn't stand at a distance and send my platitudes to do the work of being present for me. We connected because I didn't need to defend myself against the misnomer that religious belief and uncertainty cannot coexist.

It turns out that religious conversations were not a sensitive topic for Dad. Instead, my father was sensitive to overbearing, oversimplified, and dishonest proselytizing. (Everyone is, I think.) I was pleased we both lost hope in that type of religious experience. It became evident that we were both disciples on the road to Emmaus, full of lost hope, doubt, questions, and at the same time deeply needing sacred connection.

9

INNER CHILD

ACROSS FROM WHERE I SAT ON THE COUCH IN MY PARENT'S LIVING room was a newly-built entertainment center. While it featured a large TV, the shelves on either side displayed framed pictures of past family events. Weddings, college graduations, and reunions were among the memories captured. I scanned some of the pictures as my mind drifted.

Dad was sitting in his chair with a blanket covering his legs even though it was quite warm. Mom was moving about the kitchen.

"You doin' okay . . . you need something?" Dad asked, breaking me from my thoughts.

"I'm okay . . . just remembering some of these old times," I said, pointing toward the pictures.

Sadly, I tried to remember other times in my life when my father asked me if I was doing okay. Surely he had. I chalked it up to one of those things that we just don't take notice of.

But what else hadn't I noticed? What else had I missed?

"Don't worry about me, Dad. I'll help myself if I need anything."

Dad and I talked for hours on that Thursday. We had penetrated deeper into the long-hidden truths of our lives more than we had ever done together. But I was still surprised with my father's response to my comment because it opened the door to talk about our distant, unhealthy relationship.

"Worry? I won't. But for the record I've always worried myself sick, especially when you were in elementary school. All the way into adulthood," he said.

At the mention of school, a scene from twenty-five years ago flashed in my mind. On that day, I had been acting unruly at school, so Dad doled out the punishment when I got home.

"Turn around! Hands on the bed!" Dad shouted. I gripped the side of the bunkbed and looked over my shoulder in horror. He didn't take his eyes off me. With one hand he loosened his buckle, yanked the belt diagonally away from his body, and in one fell swoop, it snapped across my rear.

Mom and Dad had an agreement: he would discipline for behavioral issues at school and she would take care of the rest. I was sent to the principal's office regularly, which is a teacher's last resort in dealing with unruly students. At least once a semester, I'd spend a day with my hands folded and my head hung within eyesight of the principal. That meant the same terrible belt-whipping scene unfolded at home each semester.

It was never one whipping it was usually five. The first and second swings were to calibrate speed and accuracy. The third swing was the first one that counted, which was why my father always paused for a moment and reiterated, "We *do not* tolerate behavior like this at school!" The fourth was not so much punishment for misbehavior but a consequence for damaging the family reputation. "Fasanis don't act like that," he would say. Sometimes a fifth swing was needed for "good measure," which I believe is what disciplinarians name their unrestrained anger.

In a way, our relationship was framed by the consequences for bad behavior at school. There was never any instruction or conversation. We didn't discuss possible solutions or strategies to curb the impulse to act out. The smack of the belt, coupled with his anger, was my point of contact with Dad. It was the only real connection we had. Despite the pain, at least I had his undivided attention.

I understood the consequences for my actions. Misbehavior at school resulted in a whipping at home. That wasn't a difficult equation to grasp. What I didn't understand was the correlation between what was behind my behavior at school and why it made Dad so angry. I was craving affirmation, genuine connection, someone to tell me that I was valuable and a gift. By clowning around in the classroom, I could evoke laughter from thirty classmates. My peers temporarily met those needs.

But a child who is hit doesn't only resent the hitter. A child resents the cause of the abuse, which is not a person but the totality of the conditions that allow it to happen. I resented my father, but I also resented myself for allowing it, even though I simultaneously felt incompetent to avoiding it. And I resented life itself for delivering the pain, which fed into me a feeling of being disconnected, alone, and in need of affirmation. It was cyclical and unhealthy. And my father had the power to break the cycle but chose not to.

That third grader in need of affection and affirmation still lived inside me. That boy who continued to act out in school sat on the couch next to my father that Thursday. When Dad said he worried about me at school, I heard a cry of regret. I was learning that my father's language of love was worry.

I didn't need an elaborate apology. All I needed was for Dad to name that more was going on than my misbehavior. In other words, all I needed was my father to relieve me of the responsibility of my own whipping. I realized that his words—"I worried sick about you"—was his way of saying that he worried about me because he loved me. In that moment, a burden was lifted.

"Ryan, I worry about your work and salary daily, but I've realized I don't have to anymore. Maybe I never did. I've learned that you are good at whatever you do."

I sat there, speechless.

Four months before my visit with my father, I stepped away from a senior pastoring position in Hawaii and moved to Idaho.

My wife and I decided that for one whole calendar year, I would intentionally rest. Early January marked about one-third of the way through my year off. My unemployment, and perhaps not actively looking for a job, was a recipe for worry for Dad. He touched all the critical topics—work, salary, investments, and even a bit about retirement—but only briefly. Those topics were a means to something else he wanted to say. The conversation about work was a way for him to finally make an admission: he loved me, but he no longer needed to worry about me.

Who is this man across from me? I thought. *Where is my stoic, closed off father? Where is all this sensitivity and emotion coming from, and what on earth do I do with it?*

I just stared at him. And relished in it.

He continued, "You've always been so gifted, Ryan."

Not only was my father making admission and sharing his feelings—two things I was witnessing for the first time—he was also doling out compliments. Something wasn't right, unnatural. I tempered my euphoria with disbelief. I didn't say a word, but I imagine the expression on my face said, *Thank you, Dad, but are you losing your mind?*

"Pound for pound, you're one of the best athletes I've ever seen," he exclaimed.

It's been years since I've heard that phrase: "pound for pound." I'm rarely the smallest person in a room anymore, but as a young teen, everyone, including the girls, were bigger than me. In team pictures for football, I was in the front row, where the shortest and lightest players stood. Basketball team pictures were the same. While the tall players stood in the back row, I sat on a chair in the center front holding a ball—the place reserved for the smallest player. The same was true for baseball. At fourteen, I decided to only play one sport. When I told my parents I wasn't going to try out for the baseball team, my father looked at me in a rare moment of sincerity and said, "Pound for pound, you're one of the best athletes I've ever seen." It was his way of saying that he supported my decision but he hoped size wasn't a factor.

It was so meaningful to hear those words all these years later. It was an anchoring to a shared memory. And then it dawned on me, the double meaning of that phrase. Dad was saying two things at once: I've *always* been here, and I've *always* believed in you. It felt like I was receiving more affirmation in those few moments than the sum total of my entire childhood. A son never loses an appetite for a father's affirming words, so I feasted.

"I used to worry about you becoming a pastor. And here you've done so well. And I worried about you and Bohdana. Your marriage and family have made me proud. Ryan, I'm proud of you."

My mouth and stomach stuffed full of affirmation, I mumbled, "Um, thank you, Dad."

That's it? I talked for a living, and that was it? I had no other words in that moment.

Two voices competed for my attention. One voice told me to fly, to soar! It said, *This is a moment of weightlessness and elation, so catch the wind of affirmation and drift toward the clouds, toward the heaven you dreamed of as a child.* The other voice told me not to move, to keep my butt on the couch. *This is a moment of fleeting affirmation, exposing the severity of the moment. The darkness will soon envelope this flicker of light.*

My inner child has the capacity for innocence, inspiration, awe, and playfulness, among other childlike experiences. But that child also bears the wounds and scars of parental abuses, criticisms, and neglect. What happened when I was six or ten years old still bears on me today. My inner child is subordinate to my conscious adult self, and I cannot unlearn or un-experience my childhood.

My whole life I've craved jumping into Dad's lap and being tickled and hugged. That boy deeply desires to be seen and heard, loved and affirmed, in all his awkward antics and curiosities. Now, I was thirty-five and balding, but it felt like my dad was looking into the innocent eyes of his six-year-old son as he said, "I see you, you are okay, you are loved. Come here and let me hold you."

The boyish voice within was saying, *It's okay to let yourself be enveloped in this love and levitate, even fly.* My ego also had an opinion: *This is unfamiliar and likely fleeting, so stay seated.* The voices were that distinct. The boy in me wanted to fly. Perhaps in fear of being let down, my ego took to a defensive posture and insisted I should stay put and let it pass.

I ignored the voice that told me to stay seated, and I listened to the one that told me to catch the wind of affirmation and fly. I got a running start, jumped, and flew.

The light in the living room began to change as the sun fell toward the horizon. My father looked tired, and it was nearing dinnertime. I thanked him for his honesty, specifically for opening up about depression, and told him I was going to take a walk outside. I realized when I put weight on my feet, the flying sensation I had in my heart was also in my body. I felt lighter and more free. I walked toward the door and located my shoes. When I looked back at Dad, reclining in his blue chair, his eyes were closed, and though his body seems almost lifeless, a certain pressure was relieved from his face. I could almost make out a grin on his pale lips. I opened the door and slipped out.

Maybe it was the dark that was descending while I walked, but the thought of death hit me hard only minutes after I left Dad's living room. As if life didn't care my inner child was soaring and

I was finally building a relationship with my father, death would win. My father was going to quietly step off the stage of life and disappear behind the curtain, never to be seen again.

The inner boy in me was now having to bear too much to fly. The reality of crucifixion scolded me down from the clouds. I'd have to let go of this elation for good; this was all temporary.

Death was near, darkness would set in soon.

My hope was lost.

III

TAKING A RISK

[Jesus] asked them,
"What are you discussing
together as you walk along?"

— LUKE 24:17

1 0

BENT DOWN

WITH THE GOALS OF HELPING MY FATHER SLEEP, I STAYED AT MY brother Rocky's house, which is only a football-field-length from my parents' house. Early Friday morning before any stir in his house, I slipped out for a jog. Sound bites from my Thursday conversation with Dad echoed in my mind as I ran. The loudest echo was the "five years of hell." I still was shaken that all these years he held in the truth of his depression.

Something I had read recently from Robert Bly resonated with my reflections about my father. Bly said that what we repress in our lives gets put in a big invisible bag that we drag behind us. It's a kind of heavy shadow that not only slows us down but has surprising power over us. It requires time and energy to lug the bag, and most people will do the work of dragging it rather than the work needed to search through it for understanding. The latter is the only way to lighten the load.[1]

Dad was conservative.

This was true of his political persuasion, but I mean it more in terms of his mode of living. Small decisions or larger ones, Dad researched meticulously so as to make the safest commitment. Financially speaking, he was reserved and took very few risks. Regarding his career, he chose something predictable and steady. As a father, he gave safe, predictable advice.

I only recently threw away the manila folder titled "Roth IRA." Dad gave it to me when I was eighteen. "It's the safest investment you'll ever make," he'd said. Dad was conservative and safe, cautious about change, and never took a gamble. He was also a perfectionist.

For thirty-five years, he wore the same style of collared shirts and Dockers slacks to work, parting his hair with precision, perfectly shaven, and not a minute late. He had impeccable handwriting, excellent grammar, and was very articulate. My dad possessed all the telltale signs of a perfectionist.

Some of the more unique traits to this day bring me a smile. For example, his tools were off limits, for they needed to remain in perfect condition and properly organized, even if they sat unused for years. He tirelessly raked leaves into piles around the yard, swept walkways and driveways clear of blemishes, and piled debris cylindrically. When he walked, his white t-shirt was tightly tucked into his pants and his matching white socks were pulled taut to the identical height on both calves. His appearance, his work, and his recreation were perfect.

Dad's conservative bent and his perfectionism were closely linked. His big invisible bag was so full that he developed two huge muscles to lug perfectionism and conservatism around. Inside that bag was the immensely heavy fear of failure.

Doing things perfectly gave Dad a sense of control, and being conservative limited the unpredictability in the process. Unfortunately, while they were both attempts to stave off dealing with failure, it actually increased the likelihood of it. Raising his expectations to impossible levels inevitably raised the frequency of not reaching them, thereby increasing his failure. While Dad was trying to cope with his fear of failure, he was feeding his experience of it all along.

The dreaded outcome of failure is *not* doing something a second time or having to accept second best. The dreaded outcome of failure is shame and judgment. And instead of questioning the logic of shame or judgment (or why they are triggers for fear), Dad would internalize them, trying harder to be perfect, more consistent, safer. This is an addictive cycle that hoisted more into his invisible bag of repression.

Sigmund Freud, the father of psychoanalysis, said that what we repress by day will haunt us by night.[2] This was literally true for Dad. We're all guilty of being overly concerned about trivial things, but my father would experience full-blown anxiety. The faucet in the master bathroom was the wrong model, the railing on the porch was not finished, the road was too soft for the gravel truck to drive on, and the washer and dryer was misaligned. Every inch, every nail, every detail had to be perfect or anxiety struck.

With immense loss of sleep, Dad had become a living tomb. I was beginning to wonder if the severe anxiety he suffered, which was a symptom of repressed fear of failing, was as much an influence on his deterioration as the physiological symptoms of his disease. Insomnia is not only a struggle at night; it wracks the body at sunrise. Dad had psychological monsters that haunted him by night and physically abused his body all day.

Dad's fear of failing had manufactured a lie, one that he perpetually chased: perfection is possible. The lie has more than one layer. The first is that there is such a thing as perfection, which of course there is not. The second is that should Dad attain the impossible, he would experience satisfaction or security or both. These lies promised freedom from having to confront the fear of shame and judgment that comes with failing. The lie of perfection was in a very real way Dad's hope for salvation. Perfection was his liberation from the weight of the big invisible bag, from the monsters, from the judgment.

Unfortunately, all salvation promises are a lie at some level insofar as they are an *escape from* as opposed to an *engagement with* our true selves. Promises of fulfillment and satisfaction, extended life and increased beauty, freedom and wealth, and even perpetual rest and eternal utopia, are all salvation promises that are found in plenty today. Their implicit message is that there is the possibility of escaping our repressed fears and self-destructive behaviors.

These lies—like the lies Dad believed would free him from failure—ultimately return void. Freedom is found in sorting through, wrangling with, and confronting the big invisible bag we all carry around. Dad strove for perfection and made safe decisions to the very end. They returned void. He was still anxious.

Cleopas and his brother's salvation promises returned void too. Their conviction to follow Jesus and the new redemption movement of Israel was at its core a desire to escape their repressions, but it proved to be empty and a lie. Did they believe that the Messiah would free them from the harsh realities of their lives that they swallowed and never confronted? Perhaps Jesus, as the stranger on the road, was re-entering their lives to begin opening their big invisible bags of anxiety, fear, and repressions. Perhaps Jesus chose a long walk and conversation as an opportunity to expose the brothers' misplaced hope of circumventing the harsh realities of their inner lives. The brothers on the road to Emmaus had a big invisible bag to sort through.

Dad needed to sort through his bag as well.

SCRIPTURE BEGINS WITH THE PHRASE, "In the beginning, God created." It's not long before God steps off the heavenly throne and into the Garden of Eden. God walked with Adam and Eve. According to scripture, God has a habit of walking with people and entering the sphere of human existence. This is the definition of incarnation in Jesus: God entered the world in human likeness. God literally took on flesh (*in-carnate*).

While humans spend their time dreaming of heavenly things, God puts on flesh and gets God's hands dirty on Earth. This is one of the ironic pillars of Christianity. There are many implications of such a belief, but one that strikes me as particularly meaningful is the biblical mandate to be like God (Matthew 5:48). In one way, to be like God is a mandate to be more human—fully who we are, with others in who they are.

Many years ago, a teacher of mine, Dr. Michael Lodahl, drew my attention to a peculiarity of the ministry of Jesus. He did not detail the latest New Testament scholarship or rely on his philosophical acumen. Though especially brilliant, it was not the profundity of Dr. Lodahl's insight that has stuck with me all these years; it was the simplicity of it. He simply pointed out the posture of Jesus' ministry. Jesus was always bending over, stooping to be with children, to touch lepers, to make healing salves out of the material of the earth.[3] This is all consistent with a God that takes on materiality and bends down to a world that needs healing. To embody that divinity is to bend down and be like that God.

The bent-down Jesus reminds us that God is in the physical presence of one another, in the closeness and vulnerability of love. There's no bulletproof glass that separates the fallibility of humanity and God. There is flesh, and sometimes that flesh is broken open. There are emotions, and sometimes those emotions spill all over the people within range. God is in the *real* mess of *real* lives. That's risky business because it's unpredictable and bound to be messy. An immanent God that comes close is a God that takes risks.

I came up to Dad's house after breakfast on Friday. He was in his recliner with his feet propped up and his socks off. Mom was sitting on a stool and massaging lotion onto his dry, swollen, cracked feet. I saw the God that comes close, bends down, and rubs shoulders with humanity that morning.

In the very act of holding Dad's swollen foot, Mom offered the gentle touch of divinity to one who suffered. I silently watched, relishing in the sanctity of this healing moment. Mom wiped his feet clean with a towel, then quietly left the room.

"She's pretty amazing, huh, Dad?"

"Yeah, she's really something," he sincerely agreed.

"That's what God looks like . . . that's what grace looks like," I blurted.

"I understand that," he said.

I wasn't expecting his response, but I do believe he understood, not because he had religious training or church experience, but precisely because he *didn't.*

For many evangelical Christians, *grace* is merely a word in a long lexicon of religious language. Many pastors in my life defined *grace* as "receiving what we do not deserve." This definition has at least two meanings in my experience. The first, in classic evangelical nomenclature, is the receiving of forgiveness of sins. God, as Divine Judge, relieves me, a lowly lawbreaker, of the consequences of my actions.

The second meaning is that our material possessions are undeserved gifts. God, as Divine Gift Giver, gives me, an undeserving creature, material abundance. In both cases, grace is something we define in a way that helps us understand (and justify) our life of comfort, protected from the litany of threats to well-being and health. Consequently, grace becomes the word we use to describe the breadth of experiences associated with a desirable life: health, wealth, and happiness.

But Dad was dying, so he was looking back on a life riddled with seasons of despair, bouts of loneliness, and years of anxiety. The evangelical concept of grace simply didn't fit. There was no comfort, no health, no well-being for Dad. Instead, he was haunted by his past and quickly approaching the inevitable end of crucifixion.

Grace is not a word that defines and justifies our comfort; it's but the presence of a bent-down God in the midst of pain, which is potentially uncomfortable for those living in comfort. To the suffering, the downcast, the crucified, grace has flesh on it. Grace is, quite simply, *loving presence*. Dad was unencumbered by a self-soothing, self-justifying definition of grace. He understood a richer grace because he experienced it in the unwarranted solidarity and unconditional love of a bent-down wife.

The stranger on the road to Emmaus asked, "What are you discussing" (v17)? We miss the meaning of this question if we think the stranger is asking about the content of their conversation. When a teenager spouts, "What's for dinner?" the teenager is first making an affirmation and second an announcement. The affirmation is that the father is the chef and is expected to prepare the meal. The announcement is that the teen is hungry. The content of the coming meal is perhaps a tertiary concern. When the stranger spouted out his first question on the road, he, too, was stating an affirmation and making an announcement. The affirmation was that the men were clearly hurting, and the announcement—a publicizing of an intention—was that he'd like to join them on their walk.

The content of the brothers' conversation was not their primary concern either. It was a time of catharsis, and catharsis is concerned mostly with emotional safety. When sharing in a group, there are primary and secondary concerns. A primary concern: *Am I safe to share? Can I be vulnerable?* The content —*What should I share?*—is secondary. For the disciples, it clearly was a safe place to share, as they "talked and discussed these things with each other" (v14). Their cathartic conversation *in safe company* served as consolation in grief, a salve for their souls.

The stranger was not interviewing the brothers, nor was he primarily interested in the details of their conversation. The stranger was affirming the brothers' pain and in so doing was naming an essential truth. What they were discussing is less important than the fact that they could discuss and share in each other's hurt.

The stranger, who was later revealed as Jesus, was looking for a way to affirm their pain and ask if he could enter that suffering with them. He was acting consistent with the God that makes a habit of bending down into the hurt of humanity and being present, extending grace, and offering a bit of heaven on Earth. Literally, to be like God is to be more fully human—fully who we are in our pain, and fully with others in who they are in their pain.

EVERY YEAR we burned an annual bonfire on my birthday. When a bonfire rages, with flames that reach skyward fifty feet, there is an optimal distance to stand just close enough to feel its warmth but far enough to flee if a problem arises. Another interesting thing about a bonfire is that no one has to be encouraged to watch. Everyone stares when several cubic yards of brush ignite. It's a fireworks show, only natural.

When I was younger, my parents' marriage was like those birthday bonfires. It was essential to keep at a healthy distance and impossible not to stare. Should it get out of hand, which it often did, fleeing for safety was the best recourse.

It's no wonder I never talked to Dad about how to succeed in marriage. My comment about Mom's care for him as a display of grace was the prompt he needed, and it was our *first and only* conversation about marriage. He made several confessions and several affirmations. The former were comments about his failures as a husband and the latter acknowledged Mom's steady love for him.

"I really didn't do a good job as a husband. I was too damn stubborn. I always had to be right, and I never gave in, even the small issues," Dad confessed.

"Yup," was my insensitive verbal translation of what I was thinking: *Yeah, that sure was evident.*

"But your mother put up with me. All those years and she put up with my stubbornness."

Confession. Affirmation. Dad was stubborn; Mom was patient. The dichotomy was a bit drastic.

I offered, "Mom was stubborn too, yeah?"

Dad agreed but wasn't interested in leveling the playing field. "Yeah, which is how we stuck it out. But it wasn't easy. I'm glad we did." He took a moment to gather his bearings. "Oh, I regret how I was all those years. We had so much on our plate, and I wouldn't budge. We couldn't see eye to eye, so I did it my way."

I nodded, urging him to continue.

"That's not how you have a good marriage. You have to compromise. I really regret not compromising, not budging, at least a little, on most things," he said. While he gave me advice, it seemed it was another vehicle to reiterate his mistakes. He was obstinate and uncompromising. He could see that now; he could name that now.

I added, "Every hill was a hill to die on, it seemed."

"Yeah, every hill! Oh, but your mom would put up with it. She stuck it out. She's strong! We almost didn't make it a few times, you know. Don't ever let it get to that, Ryan. Work out those issues. Let Bohdana know you will compromise. I didn't ..."

"Oh, I know," I said.

"She's really taking care of me," Dad said. "All those years I failed and she's doing everything for me. I wouldn't make it without her." He looked to me for acknowledgement and I nodded.

He said again, but this time with a look of disappointment, "I really was difficult. I really was so hard on your mother. She put up with me all those years. She was always faithful."

Confession. Affirmation. There they were side by side again. I could tell he was drawing a connection between the two but it was muddled.

"She helped me finally realize how hard I made it on her."

The correlation between his confession of failure and his affirmation of my mother became explicit. Specifically, Mom's love and fidelity was not only a contrast to Dad's failure, it was integral to him becoming self-aware. Throughout the years, but most potently in the last year, Mom's love massaged open his eyes and he was able to see his own stubbornness and brokenness.

Divine love is not condemning or indicting, but patient and present. It sits in the mess of life, bent down, awaiting awareness. This love is risky because it waits rather than rushes, and it bends down instead of standing at a distance. It's risky because it is graceful, not coercive, and always open to rejection.

In a circuitous way, in our conversation about marriage, Dad and I were building a fuller definition of grace: the presence of love that opens one's eyes to brokenness. Mom offered that Divine love, modeled that grace, and Dad's eyes were opened. Specifically at the end, Mom took Divine, grace-full risk in caring for Dad.

The stranger on the road to Emmaus took a similar risk; he purposefully entered into the volatility and messiness of the two men. God bent down that day, and the stranger offered Cleopas and his brother grace, waiting for their eyes to open.

Dad offered me one final admonition on love in marriage, but given our conversation, it was a proclamation about grace too: "Ryan, don't wait as long as I did to experience it."

I said with both love and grace in mind, "I won't, Dad. I haven't."

11

SPACE BETWEEN US

PETER ROLLINS, A PHILOSOPHER AND THEOLOGIAN, TELLS THE tale of a woman near the dawn of the printing press who received a vision from God to translate, print, and distribute the Bible. She sold her possessions and began raising money. She had raised copious amounts of money when disaster struck her town twice. Both times she gave all of her funds to the emergency relief efforts. The third time, she was elderly, and she finally raised enough to begin the printing. It is said that *all three times* she successfully distributed the Word of God, the first two being the more beautiful.[1]

As a long-time Christian, my mother carried with her the responsibility of explaining the scriptures to Dad. She acknowledged this responsibility on many occasions, and it often bore heavily on her. But like the woman in Rollins's story, the responsibility is fulfilled differently than one might expect.

Can we speak of scripture sufficiently with language?

Can we hear it fully with ears? Certainly not.

If we try, we will always explain something that falls short of divine. God's Word, like friendship or love, needs flesh to be communicated and incarnated. Scriptures can only be properly shared insofar as they are lived, and only understood insofar as they are seen. The Word of God is not the ink, nor the binding, nor the covers that we use to encase our bibles. The Word is inspired by the very lives that embody its meaning, translating its truth through gestures of love and justice. The responsibility of sharing the scriptures was fulfilled in Mom's steadfast love and shared suffering with Dad.

With this understanding, the meaning of scripture is less contingent on articulation and more on application. Using language to explain scripture has an inherent safety valve: it can be done without practice. Incarnating scripture is risky by the sheer fact that it requires one's body, time, and resources. Jesus took this risk, and so did my mother.

Jesus began with the prophets and explained all of the scriptures to them (v27). But he explained the scriptures on the heels of insult—calling the disciples foolish and slow to understand (v25). That seems strangely insensitive for one who prefers the posture of bending down in compassionate service. The disciples were suffering tremendous loss, so why add insult to injury?

If explaining the scriptures is reduced to a verbal practice intended for intellectual apprehension, then it is insulting. But if consideration is given to a fuller meaning of "explaining the scriptures"—expressing the meaning through embodying it— then perhaps Jesus was up to something else. The verbal explanation of the scriptures wasn't his primary task. Solidarity was! The meaning of those very scriptures was "explained" by the one who bore the wounds of crucifixion and stood *with* those who mourned.

Think of it this way: Jesus was not insulting their intellect but instead drawing their attention to the fallacious tendency to think verbal communication and intellect are sufficient channels of understanding the Word of God. I imagine Jesus shaking his head as he explained the scriptures, knowing the redundancy of such a task. For the scriptures were already explained in their midst, in the one who fully embodied their meaning. His mangled body was the incarnate truth of scripture. The explanation of prophecy merely corroborated that truth.

Similarly, Mom's first task was to embody the meaning of scripture for Dad. Any type of verbal explanation would have been redundant, or worse, insulting. She took a big risk and explained the scriptures without words. Her body, time, and her tears communicated the scriptures. Being *with* Dad communicated all the incarnate truth he needed to know. Dad *saw* and *felt* the scriptures, and therefore understood their meaning.

I AM A PASTOR, which means I'm one of the first calls people make when they face death. Whether it's the diagnosis of a terminal disease, a fatal car accident, or a miscarriage, people often reach out to a pastor. Every situation is unique, but most people are afraid of death. They fear the unknown.

When I asked if my father feared the unknown, he responded in a welcoming tone, "Yes, of course I do. I've got a lot of unanswered questions. There's a lot I don't know."

"That's understandable."

He added, "I have some unfinished business too. Gotta get that done, if I can. I'm just glad you're here. I've already talked to your brothers. I'm glad I get to talk to you."

Dad had "unfinished business" *with each son*. And that business was full of unanswered questions. Talking was not Dad's strong suit. He already admitted to me that a major failure in his marriage was being an abysmal communicator, second only to being stubborn.

That came as no surprise because even though Dad was a great conversationalist, he was terrible at sharing his feelings, expressing his needs, and generally talking about relationships. Those closest to him very seldom connected verbally. Dad had business to take care of with each son, but that business required meaningful dialogue. That was unknown territory for Dad. It was unpredictable and full of questions.

More specifically, Dad was referring to the uncertainty surrounding the last son he needed to talk to, which was me. In the space between us—he on his recliner, one emaciated leg dangling across another, and me, sitting on the couch and resting one elbow on the armrest—was a universe of unfinished business. So much inhabited that space now—some wonderful and yet some still painful. Dad had been waiting for this opportunity, but he knew it was going to be messy.

"I'm just glad you're here," he said.

And just like that, the air between us shifted.

He said, "I'm just glad you're here," but what I heard and felt in the space between us was "I just need intimacy and connection with my boys. And this is it. This is good." Dad's soul was speaking.

When we enter this world, we gain a profound sense of subjectivity. Every child loses the closeness to his or her mother, some sooner than others. We are birthed, weaned, then expected to act on our own. It's a slow process of developing independence, self-awareness, and subjectivity. We become our own. We are confronted with restrictions as soon as we are free to step onto the stage of this world. The world—the prevailing kingdom of our time—places demands on its subjects: comply, work, consume, repeat. As soon as we gain independence, we are threatened with ignoring our unique inner self and complying with the external refrain. We are threatened with living a divided life.

Parker Palmer, a writer and spiritual leader, writes extensively about living a life of wholeness and its antithesis, what he calls "the divided life." Palmer says that a life of wholeness is a life that holds the inner and outer life as one consistent whole.[2] Unfortunately, life is often lived when these two parts of a person are at odds with each other.

However, in each of us is a quiet voice that reminds us of who we are, how we are unique, and what our truth is. Too often, this voice is ignored. Our inner self—our soul that only speaks in a quiet voice but has our full attention when we're very young—slowly fades into the background. It doesn't press us to listen, nor does it scream for attention. Instead, it would prefer to wait. The consequence of living with this division is that the inner part of us that is hidden from the world eventually disappears from our awareness, perhaps never to be heard. This is a great travesty because it's only at death—or close to it—that our soul is once again free.

Dad's inner self wanted to talk meaningfully with his sons. His soul, of course, always desired that connection, but Dad was divided. Perhaps as death came closer, his soul began to shake loose. The refrain of this world that was telling him to push on, to work, and to consume, loosened its grip. Or maybe his crucifixion weakened his ability to maintain a distance between his outer world, which he could control, and his inner world, which he perceived as dangerously unpredictable. In either case, death was imminent, and Dad began listening to his soul. It was awakening, coming alive. After six decades, he was able to hear the cry of his inner self, the quiet voice inside.

Dad was experiencing wholeness, and his soul sensed freedom. Like the disciples on their way to Emmaus, the roots of the old life, the old rule, and the old Kingdom were being unearthed. Dad's inner self was burning like that of the disciples because, in all their suffering, God risked being close. I relished in our conversations. I delighted in connecting with my father. For the first time I was experiencing his wholeness, his freedom.

THE STRANGER ASKED a second question on the road to Emmaus: "What things [have happened]" (v19)? This question was an echo of the very question the brothers had been asking themselves. They were discussing all that had happened, and they were comparing experiences and sharing opinions about what happened and what would ramify. History told this way is not about facts as much as it's about one's subjective relationship to events. History told this way is always ideological in nature, for it tells a story of events *from a particular perspective.* In other words, it reveals as much about the one experiencing the event as it does about the factors and forces influencing the event itself.

Cleopas and his brother answered the stranger, and it was revealing: "The chief priests and our rulers handed [Jesus] over to be sentenced to death, and they crucified him" (v20). The brothers had given their entire lives to the dawning of the new Kingdom, as taught by Jesus the Nazarene, but they had yet to expel the dominion of the old kingdom from within. The rulers who were responsible for their grief were not foreign rulers of the Roman Empire but "*our* rulers" (emphasis added). The two men fully accepted Roman rulership.

Rome was not just in political control of the Judean countryside; Rome was in ideological control of the Jewish imagination. Rome had ascended to the highest form of superiority in Jewish self-understanding. God was not the ruler of these two men, Rome was. Jesus and his message of a new Kingdom had not yet uprooted the belief that Roman soldiers were ultimately in control of their fate and that Rome owned their future.

On that walk, the not-yet-revealed Jesus went to work uprooting the former kingdom deeply established within them. The word *heart*, for Luke, is the "location" where ideology and self-understanding collide. The *heart* is where opposing kingdoms collide (Luke 16:13). The collision is explicit—it surfaces, manifesting in conflict—throughout Luke's telling of the story.

The brothers said one thing, but felt another in their heart. They embodied the conflict! They revealed the ideological control Rome had successfully impressed on them (v20), but their hearts burned with the awareness that a different truth was possible (v32). Jesus took a risk to free these two men from lost hope and ideological bondage, and it was beginning to work.

My entire morning with Dad was an extended surprise, from Mom massaging Dad's feet to Dad's transparency. But the thing that surprised me most was the pervasive openness Dad had to my presence. We spent hours sitting, talking, and connecting. I was used to a father who displayed his stress as irritability. By Friday, that changed, and he was undergoing a dramatic transformation.

What was this transformation?

After thirty years, what had changed to make room for my extensive presence?

I needed some fresh air and wanted to scribble down a few notes from our conversation. "Do you mind if I go for a little walk?" I asked.

"Of course not," he said. "This was good. I enjoyed it. Will you come back this afternoon?"

A fundamental belief that a father and son could not emotionally connect and be truly transparent was being uprooted. I experienced it between us. Like the disciples, it was ultimately the burning in our hearts that would prove our former beliefs invalid. The burning in Dad's heart was confirmation that he was undergoing a major transformation.

As I walked around the property, I was aware that Dad's heart was changing, and I knew why. God was close, serving him, rubbing his feet, and sharing in his suffering. Scripture was being experienced and explained along the way.

CONVERSION

In Mother Teresa's autobiographical letters, *Come Be My Light*, she shares with candor about three "conversions."[1] As I understand them, her first conversion compelled her to give up her whole life for the purpose of serving God and others. She embodied this conversion by committing to a life of poverty, give up all that makes life comfortable and convenient, and serving the poor in Calcutta, India.

Her second conversion didn't demand a material change but it was no less profound. It required that she give up on feeling God's presence and accept an empty abyss that God once filled. She converted from needing to feel God's presence to knowing that God's presence is not always felt. This conversion was marked by dryness, desolation, and darkness.

Her third conversion was the discovery of God. She did not discovery a new God as much as she discovered God in a *new place*: in the darkness. She found God in the very wounds of the dying. She discovered God in the darkness, the depression, the pain from within. She embraced the subjectivity and pain and broken personhood of the other.

The Christmas Eve email I wrote to Mom and Dad in the wake of the ALS diagnosis was a proclamation that God comes close in times of suffering. Christmas is the reminder of that divine truth in the form of the Christ child. I wrote:

> On Christmas Eve we shiver with the shepherds in the field and the Magi on their sojourn. We shiver with them perhaps because it was cold, but more so because we search for a God that gives up being far away and safely sheltered in heavenly distance . . . . The Creator of the heavens will labor with a young mom, deliver into the hands of a young man, cry that chilling first squeal, and nurse. The Creator is a baby, one of us, human. One of us! We're not alone. God is with us, Mom and Dad.

My letter didn't tell the whole story or my whole truth. For many months, I experienced a type of divine dryness, a divine distance. I felt a grand canyon between God and myself. It wasn't so much an impasse but more like a chasm that was big enough and dark enough to fit an enormous absence.

God labored with Mary, but I had forgotten what it felt like to experience that immanence. Despite my cognitive understanding, my body—my chest, my bones, my being— needed a type of reawakening to the God that is near and with us. By writing the email, I was proclaiming a truth to my parents *and* reiterating a truth to myself. I was reminding myself what I believe despite sensing it as untrue.

What I wrote to my parents on Christmas Eve I began to experience for the first time in months. Especially Friday morning, in Dad's presence, I felt and saw God again. There was no spectacular show of transcendent glory. I wasn't filled with chills or a strange warmth in my heart. Instead, in Dad—the one who was suffering, crucified, and emaciated—I was reminded of the closeness of God. Like Mother Teresa, after a long season of dryness, I found the Divine *in Dad's wounds.*

I questioned whether I, too, was undergoing a kind of conversion just like Mother Teresa. I wasn't experiencing a religious conversion in the way that I had learned to understand "conversion." All the dualistic, limiting language I learned to associate with conversion simply did not apply. I didn't traverse the gap between ignorance and knowing the truth. I didn't move from unbelief to belief in Jesus. I didn't shift from secular to religious.

My conversion was not an issue of eternal destiny; it was too material, too here and now. But it was a transformation, as radically altering as any conversion I had witnessed. I was experiencing something ineffable and outside the scope of evangelical language. In Dad's woundedness was a divine solidarity, and in entering those wounds, I was brought near to the God that indwells all wounds. Like Mother Teresa, I discovered God anew in the darkness.

And I was not alone in my experience.

"I love taking care of Dad," Mom told me more than once over the last few months. "I don't know what it is, but I don't mind it at all. I actually like doing it." She was undergoing a similar conversion, encountering a divine closeness. She was drawn near to Dad in his sickness, lured toward his hurt.

In those cracked feet, boney legs, and gaunt cheeks, there was a calling. God was calling her to come close. Mom's call to care for Dad was as strong as Mother Teresa's call to give up her life for service to the poor. Both women were asked to give up all that was familiar and commit to an irrational fidelity. And Mom discovered in the very pain of Dad's atrophied body that there was more than need, more than desperation and lost hope. There was literally Divine presence.

The three travelers on the road were a band of brokenness and wounds: physical, psychological, emotional. The closer the brothers drew to the wounds, the more they opened themselves and grieved together, and the longer they traveled in solidarity, the closer they drew God. What they experienced on the road to Emmaus was the same thing Mom and I experienced in Dad's living room: God indwells weak bodies and broken flesh.

IV

BIGGER RISK

But they urged him strongly,
"Stay with us, for it is nearly evening;
the day is almost over."

— LUKE 24:29

13

CONFESSION

Friday afternoon was a time of big risk-taking for Dad. He shared in ways that I had never witnessed. One such case was an abrupt and explicit admission of failure. My father was still sitting in his chair in the corner of the living room next to the window.

"I failed, Ryan," he said abruptly.

"Failed?" I blurted. I was surprised and a bit confused that he used the word *failed.*

Failure was not something we admitted to in our family. We didn't have excuses, blame others, or lie about our mistakes. Rather, we simply believed that with harder work and another chance we could get it right.

When I was in my freshman year of high school, every student was required to take a typing class one hour a day, five days a week. We would sit in front of boxy Apple computers with grainy black screens and green lettering, and crawl through a program that taught proper typing technique. That was the whole class. No teaching lessons and no interaction with other students. I was bored senseless. With my hands motionless on the keyboard, and my eyes glazed over and slightly out of focus, I'd stare at the screen, day after day. When our progress reports were sent home at the midpoint of the semester, my parents were stunned that I had five A's and an F in typing.

Discussion of failure was never brought up. My mother said one thing to me: "We don't fail." She arranged with the teacher and the custodian for me to come to school one hour early for the remainder of the semester. Ashamed for bringing home the lowest grade ever in our family and embarrassed for inconveniencing my teacher, I arrived to school at 5:45 a.m. for three months. I started the program from the beginning, and in half the time I was able to finish every assignment for the whole year. The F became an A, and I received a 4.0 that semester. *We don't fail.*

Dad's eyes dropped to the floor. "I failed a lot. A lot." There was a long, hard, silent pause, and then he continued, "I already told you about marriage, but I'm talking about failing at being a father."

I couldn't believe he'd said he failed at being a father.

"I failed *you*," he said plainly with his head hung.

There was something powerfully inviting about that statement. It was a peek into a truth I didn't think existed. Both of us held onto the same truth that he'd failed as a father. Truth—especially difficult ones—when held with humility are inviting. It drew me closer to him, closer to *his* truth.

I reciprocated, "I agree, Dad."

He looked me in the eye. "I know, I know you do."

"Why weren't you there? All I wanted was your time." I was pressing him.

Dad slowly shook his head. He had come far enough to own the truth of his failure as my father, but he wouldn't elaborate. I didn't expect him to venture far, if at all, so I was satisfied with his confession. *Maybe I shouldn't have pushed him that far,* I thought.

He was rubbing his tongue over his front teeth, bulging his upper lip as he raked it left and right a few times. He shook his head and inhaled through his nose. Then he stretched the corners of his mouth back, engaging the muscles in his cheeks and jaw, slightly exposing his teeth. It looked like a plastic smile —only the shape, none of the delight. Then he relaxed his cheeks, pressed his lips together, making them almost disappear. Tongue over teeth, plastic smile, disappearing lips. He did this several times.

Dad often did this when he was ruminating over a difficult topic. Usually it was a problem that needed solving or a decision that needed to be made. It was the routine he unconsciously followed when asked about a career change or choosing between two highly rated vehicles. It helped him process. Maybe you tap your finger on a desk or chew on your nails. I usually flip a pen between my fingers. It wasn't so much a nervous twitch, but it occupies restless muscles while thinking. It's a sign of taking something seriously, committing to the process of finding a means forward.

Dad wasn't avoiding the questions; he was working to find an answer. He was trying to put words to his difficult truth, to further explain his confession. He was looking vulnerability in the face and searching for words with which to engage it. He was not running from it, dismissing it, closing off to it. He was leaning into it. Before he uttered a word, Dad's heart was further opening up to me.

"I don't know. All I know is that I let you down."

Dad cocked his head slightly and looked at the ceiling. There was a contemplative look on his face as he searched for an explanation. But all he did was shake his head in disapproval and say, "I don't know, Ryan. I really just don't know."

Something about the third time clued me in to the deeper meaning of that repeated phrase. "I don't know" might seem like he was giving an answer without answering, but I don't believe he was being evasive. To admit he didn't know was a powerful answer in itself. It was an expression of vulnerability because it was an admission of inadequacy. It was a double admission. He owned his truth of failing, and he risked admitting he didn't know how to explain it. I'd never seen my father so vulnerable.

"Why didn't you just take me fishing?" I said, exasperated.

When I was a boy, all I wanted was for my father to take me fishing. He arranged for me to go with his friend Bob, occasionally. While that satisfied my hankering to fish, it didn't satisfy the desire to fish *with Dad.* I convinced him to come along one time. He bemoaned the trip, but I was happy just to have him. He had never seen me so much as cast, let alone hook, wrestle, catch, and release a fish. All morning and well into the afternoon we buzzed around Lake Almanor finding enticing pockets to catch bass. I'm not sure Dad looked up from reading the newspaper one time. He was in the boat with us, but I'm not sure if he was really present.

"I don't like fishing," he replied. And then he caught himself for being defensive. He quickly shifted back to a posture of confession. "And that's what I would tell myself. But that's an excuse, and a terrible one. I should have gone fishing with you. I'm so sorry, Ryan. My timing was off. It was always off. I only realized when it was too late just how much it would have meant to go fishing with you. I can see it now."

Dad's weakness was on full display, and he was exposing his complete vulnerability. But his weakness and vulnerability were not associated, as it might seem. He wore weakness like a garment that was draped over his frail body, engulfing his atrophied appendages. He couldn't get out from under it; he couldn't change. He wore weakness indefinitely.

But he *chose* his vulnerability. He chose to be vulnerable by opening himself up through admission. The vulnerability was not consuming his helpless body like physical weakness. He stepped into the vulnerability. In this case, a deliberate and strong step. His vulnerability was closer to bravery than weakness, perhaps a sign of the strength he still had hidden in the enclaves of his will.

Brené Brown has made it her career goal to start a national conversation about shame. She has stirred awareness about issues of vulnerability, fear, and emotional risk-taking. Brown says the primary myth of vulnerability is that it reveals weakness. Vulnerability is being exposed and uncertain of the outcome, which is not at all a sign of weakness. Rather, it's a sign of courage. Being vulnerable is a sign of a willingness to live fully without inhibition and with conviction.[1] Vulnerability is quite the opposite of weakness; it's risky business.

Dad took a big risk when he allowed me to see him exposed and vulnerable. He admitted failure as a father, admitted an inability to explain his actions, and apologized for realizing his mistakes later in life. Dad's admissions of guilt and apology were the strongest I had ever seen him. With his body deteriorating and weakness on full display, his strength emerged. The child within me rejoiced at seeing my father in this new light. *Dad is a risk taker. Dad is powerful.*

Dad was in good company with other risk takers. Cleopas and his brother welcomed the traveler into their chaos and the unpredictability that was their home under duress. They had already included the stranger into their conversation as they walked, but now they were inviting him to observe and participate in their private lives. They were going to be fully exposed to this man. Dad also chose to be vulnerable, and he invited me inside to look around at the chaos.

MOM CARRIED in a tray of snacks, and the smile on her face reminded me of childhood when she would offer me and my friends fresh fruit and crackers. It's funny how a gesture can transport us back in time. It all felt so long ago . . . and it was.

She placed the tray down on the end table between the couch and my father's chair. She wore every bit of exhaustion from caring for my father, but her smile assured me of her pleasure in overhearing our conversation. "Don't let me interrupt," she said, as she turned and scurried out of the living room.

"You never know what a day will bring, Ryan. Don't take any days for granted. Enjoy each one."

Of course, I nodded like everyone does when they are implored with the same platitudinous wisdom. The statement itself is meaningful but it's impractical. It never comes with a user manual. There are no YouTube tutorials on how to wake up and not take something for granted. (On second thought, maybe there are.) *Why would he feel the need to share that, at this time, more than once?* I wondered.

There must be something under that platitude worth exploring, so I went searching for it. "How do I do that?" I asked.

In a moment of pure honesty, he said, "I'm not sure."

"Well, what would you have done differently?" I asked.

"There's a lot I would have done differently." I think he was pumping the conversational brakes.

"Well, what would you have done differently if you listened to your own advice?" I grabbed a few slices of apple and some nuts off the tray.

A look of discovery overcame his face. "You know, I never just relaxed and enjoyed life . . . like I'm doing right now."

His comment prompted a list of questions. *What was he doing exactly? Was he intentionally being slippery with his answers? Am I missing something?* I was jolted into awareness. Dad was telling me that he was experiencing the very fulfillment of his own advice in that very moment.

"Do you mean you're not taking today for granted, Dad?"

"Look at me. I'm too weak to do any damn work around here. I can sit. That's it. And I'm finally being open and confessing. This is what I mean. And I'm enjoying it, Ryan!"

"Me too, Dad."

I went searching and it only took a few minutes to find. It wasn't what I was expecting. Giving impractical advice not only comes without a user manual, but it often comes from a non-user. As in Dad's case, the one who gives advice only theoretically believes it is good to practice. He had very little experience in application, if any at all.

It seemed that Dad didn't know how to avoid taking a day for granted, living each day meaningfully and to its fullest enjoyment. In theory it made sense, but in practice, he failed. He was essentially telling me, "Do as I say, not as I have done or have any idea how to do."

For Dad, taking a day for granted is to assume another day will follow. It's the mindset that joy can be postponed until tomorrow. The problem is that the same rationale can be applied tomorrow, which postpones enjoying the present yet another day. My father was a seasoned expert at missing joy in the present. And here we were enjoying today!

Dad busied himself with work and worry, to-do lists, and planning for the future so much that he never stopped or rested. Dad was always doing something, even if that doing looked like relaxing. His mind was still busy. "Doing" was always a type of foreboding joy. In the fear that something unpredictable might happen, he busied himself in preparation and planning. Doing was ostensibly a pursuit of en-*joy*-ment; it was in actuality the very thing that inhibited him from experiencing it.

Paradoxically, in the midst of suffering, Dad mysteriously experienced joy. Despite his own understanding, despite his suffering, my father stumbled upon a joy-filled experience in our time together on that Friday. His sickness was a forced stoppage. ALS was a torturous rest.

Enjoying the present happens when the "doing" stops. It happens between doing. It surprisingly manifests in the calm, during the rest. As Dad said, the building of the house was finished and his body hadn't the strength to do any more work. Though he was forced to stay put—to literally stop doing anything—he found himself in the midst of joy. Joy was able to settle into his tired body not in doing but in being still. Stop, rest, and the day will *not* be taken for granted.

Joy seems to be the gift of resting. While we can stimulate a sensation of happiness through doing, joy is more of an all-encompassing gift that we experience through "non-doing." Resting doesn't cause joy, as if joy is affected in us by "doing" rest. Instead, rest frees us from the very things that inhibit joy from settling in, such as worrying about endless lists of tasks and activities. Dad was teaching me through our time together that rest is an "un-doing" of our penchant for busyness and control.

In rest, there is real joy.

The disciples said to their fellow traveler, "The day is almost over" (v29). The day was ending, which was their justification for insisting the traveler stay with them for the night. But I wonder if there was a hint of what Dad and I experienced. Might there be the belief that a bit of joy can filter into their chaos should they stop, rest, or "turn in" for the night?

The crucifixion, the walk on the road to Emmaus, the talking . . . these were all actions, all movement, all doing. The invitation to stay, though it was risky, was the first narrative gesture toward pause. It was the first point in the story that hinted at a stoppage, at stillness. Perhaps, it was a foreshadow of a restful time and space that would allow joy to enter back into an otherwise hopeless suffering. Perhaps Luke was hinting at what I discovered with Dad, that real joy is found in rest.

14

INVITATION

The French philosopher, Emmanuel Levinas, makes a distinction between the *saying* and the *said*. Every time I speak, there's the act of *saying* and there is the content of what is being *said*.[1] An experience with a toddler can illuminate this distinction.

When my young child falls and hits his head, which seems to happen quite often, I can tell him that it's just a bump and the swelling will subside in an hour. Grammatically speaking, very little content is actually being shared through what I've *said*. But the very act of communicating is actually *saying* a tremendous amount. At the level of *saying*, I have shared the assurance that I am here with him in the pain and will comfort him until he feels better. If he rests his head on my shoulder and mumbles something unintelligible, he has *said* nothing. What he is *saying*, however, is full of meaning. He is saying that he finds comfort in me and trusts that my closeness will help him feel better.

In my time with Dad, it was important for my language—what I *said* in a Levinasian sense—not to inhibit what I was *saying*. Up until that moment with my father, I had not attempted an explanation or rationale for his suffering. Offering a theological rationale would not have provided comfort or expressed love. On the contrary, and at the level of *saying*, quite the opposite is true: not explaining, not rationalizing, and not justifying the crucifixion that is ALS allowed me to communicate more richly and more truthfully with Dad.

I didn't reference scripture, for the truth of the Bible is found in drawing close to him in his suffering. I didn't use theological language to help him understand why this awful experience might be happening, for the truly theological and truly meaningful communication was in the very act of being fully present.

Dad knew that I was trained to talk religiously, which was why he also knew the intentionality by which I abandoned that language to be more fully with him. I became vulnerably present (what I was *saying*) to be with him in his vulnerability, and I did this by throwing off the often destructive religious jargon (what I could have *said*).

Theodicy is the theological exercise of understanding evil. Generally, it is an effort in making sense out of evil and suffering. Specifically, it is the theological attempt to reconcile belief in a loving God and the experience of evil in the world. In a way, anyone verbally engaging the phenomenon of pain in this world to try to make sense of that pain is engaging in a kind of theodicy. A problem arises in most, though not all, attempts at understanding evil and suffering. While there are attempts to give explanation to suffering, what is being *said* often strips the encounter of the meaningful connections that make suffering bearable. In other words, making cognitive sense of pain runs the risk of bankrupting the resource of interpersonal connection, which makes pain bearable.

Relationships, not theories or explanations or justifications of suffering, make pain bearable. Theodicy, in times of suffering, is a retreat to the safe enclaves of the abstract. Shared pain is not a stepping away but an entering into the messy and unintelligible pain of an other. The former is rich in theory but poor in meaning; the latter is deficient of explanation but rich in understanding the nature of suffering, namely, that it's bearable *with* others.

I was fully *with* Dad in his suffering and his lost hope. I was learning that when we abandon pretense, abandon theodicy, and sit with each other in our humanity—accompanied with a lot of silence and sometimes words—we experience a richness in relationship in the midst of pain. I can only think to call it *solidarity in suffering.* And it seemed a stark contrast to the words, the concepts, the theories that would have helped explain Dad's wounds but inhibited bearing the pain of those wounds.

I suspect the stranger on the road to Emmaus communicated with the disciples as much *without* words (how he was *saying*) as he did *with* words (what he *said* about scripture). He didn't wave his scars as a banner of pride, but his way of drawing close to them, endearing himself to them in their grief, was such that his life's scars would have exposed themselves. This mystery man was but another man on the journey through life—human, hurting, grieving.

I SAT ON THE COUCH. Dad was still in his recliner-turned-convalescent-bed.

We both moved very little, but already we had journeyed much farther than I thought we ever would. We discussed memories I didn't know existed; we talked about regrets and fears and failures. We talked about marriage with a sincerity that I hadn't seen before. I was stunned with all the terrain we had covered.

Dad continued to show signs of being relaxed. His transparency was so satisfying, so refreshing. Each exchange grew my desire for more, and the situation made me aware of an appetite I didn't know I had. That's how love works, I think.

Love enables us to appreciate what we know about a person, but more importantly, we learn just how much more we are capable of knowing. I experienced genuine love on that Friday afternoon. Love exposes our ignorance of the one we love, and we're comfortable with that. Why? Because true love doesn't have a quota of understanding—it has an ever increasing capacity to know. This is why love necessarily includes mystery.

Love frees us from the confinements of propositional statements, diagrams, boundaries, and parameters. We don't relate to our beloved as something to be controlled because love is freeing. It's mysterious and big, but at the same time personal and particular. Love breaks open what we once thought was a limit, of ourselves and the other. This is part of the reason why trust is at the center of love. Love doesn't demand, confine, coerce, or control; love liberates in a way that trust comes naturally.

I experienced the mystery of my father, and I learned so much that I didn't previously know, realizing in the process that there was so much more complexity to Dad than I thought. Trust between us emerged because I learned to not put presupposed parameters around it.

"I want you to walk with me, Ryan."

"What do you mean?" I asked, confused.

"I want you to walk with me to the end. I trust you will go slowly. I don't want to go fast. I want to ask questions."

"I can't promise I have many answers, Dad. But I can promise that I will tell them straight, and I'll tell you when I don't really know."

"I just want you there with me."

"Okay, Dad. Okay."

There it was . . . trust. He trusted me to walk with him, physically, but also spiritually, on the daunting journey of death. No greater expression of trust exists than to invite someone to be at one's bedside at the end. This was a fatherly love like nothing I had ever tasted. This was a rich, true love. Trust and mystery: the two marks of genuine love.

Just one day before, I was reminded of my preconceived notion of fatherly love. It was a preformed mold of what love should look like. And I learned the hard way, through a type of growing awareness about my own ignorance, that I was missing Dad's unique form of love. I was looking for the wrong thing! It was such a relief to have the epiphany that indeed, for many years, he was loving me naturally, though in a different way than I expected. I could now experience it anew.

I learned that he loved me, but that didn't satisfy the appetite for wanting to know the mysterious father in front of me. I learned so much, and yet I hardly knew him!

The disciples allowed the stranger on the road to walk with them toward Emmaus. But when they approached their front door, despite arriving at their destination, they had not truly arrived. Their journey included but a few more feet—the most critical stretch. They were yet to traverse the threshold of the front door. They insisted that the stranger walk with them to the true end of their journey. They trusted this man and so took the risk of love by inviting him to the center of their house.

I walked with Dad all of Thursday and Friday. He trusted me and invited me to be with him not only at his bedside but also to the center of his life. He risked being with me.

MY EXPERIENCE with the dying is that there's a keen awareness between *next* and capital *N*, *Next*. There's the *next* thing that happens on the short road of life left to travel, but then there is an explicit onramp to the eternal *Next*. Dad was close to dying. My assumption is that he was very aware—even if very uncertain—of just how close his Next "life" was.

I was very careful *not* to talk about what was Next. I trusted that it would simply emerge the more Dad trusted me with the present. Evidently, Dad's trust in me grew quickly, and Next presented itself sooner than I thought. He outright said, "I'm scared. I'm afraid of what's Next." I knew immediately what he meant, not because the inflection of his voice changed to somehow indicate he was talking about eternity, but because he spoke of it *and* fear in the same sentence. In my experience, many people are *uncertain* about what the next day might bring. Most *fear* what happens in the Next "life." It seemed the same for Dad.

If Dad's vulnerability opened up space for our relationship to move forward, his willingness to admit fear allowed for a frontier of possibilities. But it wasn't a spiritual depth as one might think. To clarify, I didn't make it a spiritual depth in that I didn't assert spiritual certainty in response to his uncertainty. Dad expressed a fear of the unknown future and interest in conversing about what's Next. That did not give me license to offer prepackaged religious answers. If anything, offering religious certainty reigns in the frontier, rendering it a domesticated front yard.

Dad was afraid of the mystery that is forever, the step into that unnamable void which never ends. Even responding directly, inserting my truth, would have put restrictions on what was about to happen.

The frontier opened *because* I waited, *because* I sat in silence.

"I don't know what to think. I have a lot of questions," Dad admitted.

We sat quietly for a minute.

He added, "It scares me . . . what's Next scares me."

He looked at me as if he wanted me to respond, but again I waited. I was committed to allowing him to finish his thought.

He continued, "I don't want to be coerced into something. The problem with others is that they have all the answers. And they're pushy. I'd rather keep my questions to myself."

I waited quietly, and then I was invited into the sanctuary of Dad's life, the most protected and vulnerable part of who he was: his fear of the ultimate, uncontrollable, eternal future. And I made it past the red tape of his experience, which was "pushy" evangelism.

Like Dad, the two disciples took a risk when they invited the stranger into their chaos (their feelings and the chaos that would be their dinner table). They risked being judged, but they also risked relational solidarity. This risk, for many, is a far superior one, because it requires exposing our own woundedness and coming to grips with the wounds of others. While the benefits are potentially more lasting, the risks are potentially more far reaching. The benefit can be genuine acceptance and friendship; the risk is someone knowing the darkness of who you really are. For the disciples, their chaos became an opportunity, albeit a risky one, for solidarity and lasting friendship.

Dad took the same risk.

***

EVANGELISM SIMPLY MEANS BEARING good news, taken from the Latin word, *euangelion.* Pushy evangelism, however, is a *bad* experience and is not evangelism at all. It's bad news. It's coercion.

In my experience, the idea of hell—some form of eternal isolation—is better than a life full of disingenuous false connection. Unfortunately, the latter is often offered to the suffering under the guise of evangelism. False connection is the "comfort" that one offers the suffering in the form of easy answers or quick fixes while failing to be present in any meaningful way. False connection is ostensibly offering good news from a distance. "Comfort" of this kind is fundamentally avoidance; it does not require courage, but is instead cowardice.

The best news for the suffering is not an easy answer. The best news for the one who suffers is the assurance that someone can stand close to the suffering itself and be comfortable with the mystery and anguish of it.

Being close to pain and not being able to fix or rationalize it is incredibly disempowering, which is exactly why so many attempt to avoid it. Applying religious clichés is one way of avoiding proximity to suffering. Most evangelism demands knowing the answer, offering the solution, and thereby never stands close enough to the suffering to be remotely considered intimate. This is why in the face of the anguish of suffering and death, answer-oriented evangelism hoists hell rather than heaven onto the dying.

True evangelism, in which news that is genuinely good is offered, is contingent on interpersonal connection. Evangelism of this nature fosters a connection by way of drawing close to the one who suffers and gently holding the mystery, not running from it or forcing it to make sense. Consequently, evangelism works backwards in two ways.

The common assumption is that the Good News of Jesus the Christ is something brought, often through words, to the suffering other. Contrarily, the Good News *occurs* through compassionate and often silent presence with the hurting other. And the more faithfully one can be present, listen, and serve the hurting, the more likely the Word will become flesh (John 1:14).

Out of the mystery of suffering, an incarnate truth emerges and is experienced.

Evangelism works backwards in that the closer we get to the experience of suffering in the other, the more a picture of ourselves is reflected back to us. In the pain and humanity of the sufferer, we find our very own weakness and humanity. With our humanity in plain sight, mutuality becomes possible. The Good News is good because it manifests in the solidarity between mutuals.

The more I sat with Dad—incapable of mending my father's wounds, unwilling to offer him easy spirituality—the more I saw my own uncertainties and my own fears. I chose to look into his eyes and into his wounds. I felt the temptation to offer advice, to put his frailty into eternal perspective. It's enticing, but it's also disengaging.

I chose to engage and to be close and to maintain the intimacy with silence. The more I was genuinely present, the further he risked and welcomed me in. We were both experiencing authentic evangelism—*the* Good News of solidarity, in our rawness, in our weakness, in our humanity. We were, I imagine, experiencing the same solidarity that was experienced between the wounded stranger and the wounded disciples on the Emmaus Road. And the disciples also welcomed the stranger in.

Even further and more specific to my evangelical Christian upbringing, true evangelism ruptures the very concept of evangelism in contemporary Christian circles. The goal of evangelism simply cannot be the movement from unbelief to belief, from not knowing what's Next to knowing and accepting entrance into heaven. That is terrible news for one who is less in need of knowledge and belief and more in need of love. In loving and compassionate presence in the face of suffering, there is only room for an invitation for genuine connection.

This is why true evangelism not only ruptures our understanding of offering heaven to the other, but it often reverses the roles entirely. The evangelizer—the one bearing the message of truth—becomes the evangelized. The healthy evangelizer is often converted: he is moved from believing his answers matter to knowing his answers are not needed. Even further, the evangelizer is moved from bringing what he thought was the Good News to the suffering other to experiencing the Good News with the sufferer in the face of so many unknowns.

Dad wasn't explicitly evangelizing, but I was certainly experiencing a kind of conversion. I was converting to a new understanding and new experience of the Good News.

Same Jesus. Same God. Same Good News.

But the roles were reversed.

15

REDEMPTION

I'VE LONG BELIEVED THAT SOCIAL MEDIA IS A PROJECTION OF OUR idealized selves. It's inherent to the platform. It serves as the canvas where we paint exactly the life we want the world to think we are living. We post the pictures that show our best features and conveniently leave out the ones where we look the most unbecoming. We retweet the quotes that reflect on us well and delete the ones that give the wrong impression.

Social media is not simply an idealized version of our real life but instead a projection of a projection. The very lives we are living—the clothes we wear, the events we attend, the people we relate to, the house we furnish—are not a perfect reflection of who we really are. Our lives are a projection of the life we want to be living.

The act of hosting guests is a good example of our real life and the façade. Hosting helps us understand that our normal lives are an attempt to live out who we want to be but really are not. This is why welcoming guests is a risk. First, hosting brings into focus the truth that we often manufacture the lives we live. For example, we tidy things up to the desired cleanliness that we want to portray to others. We want our guests to perceive us as clean. We may want to be a perpetually clean and tidy person, but we're not that person. The threat, of course, is that something is missed, maybe a stain is overlooked or curtains and pillows don't match. Consequently, the truth is out and our projection is manufactured and temporary.

Second, we risk exposing our true self in hosting. It exposes just how different we really are from the life we live. Someone in our home is capable of seeing this discrepancy, and the discrepancy may reveal a truth about us that we'd rather hide. In other words, we run the risk of being exposed for who we *really* are in all our messiness and madness.

The third risk of hosting is the biggest risk of all. In the very receiving of guests we run the risk of revealing our true self to *us.* Sometimes the one my true self is most thoroughly hidden from is me. It sounds strange, but it is quite common. We manufacture a projection of ourselves so that we don't have to deal with the inner self that begs for our attention. We literally create our environment in such a way, so we lose the ability to distinguish fiction from fact, the projection from the inner truth.

This third risk is denial. Many people I've talk to don't believe social media is an idealized projection of who they really are. They think they are who their Facebook wall says they are. They've literally become their own deceived audience. When we host, we run the risk of cracking the fragile walls of our contrived reality, revealing that there is more to who we are than what we have worked so hard to create.

Cleopas and his brother invited Jesus to stay, and they became hosts. They risked in all the ways previously mentioned. Many of us tidy up before we welcome guests. Our guests come in through the front door, make their way to the living room (that usually has toys strewn about), and sit on the couch (that only gets vacuumed when guests are over). We take a risk, and in general, it works without hiccup. The two disciples didn't have this luxury. They arrived at the same time as their fellow traveler. No warning, no time to hide the mess.

Jesus entered the impromptu, uncut messiness of their lives. They were inevitably going to be exposed in the first two ways. The third risk—the truth about ourselves being revealed to us— would have to wait. Would the very presence of the guest serve as a mirror to the discrepancies between their inner selves and the people they portrayed themselves to be?

Dad was hosting in those final few days. He risked in the same way that the disciples risked. He hadn't the energy to tidy things up so as to give the impression his life was in order. His brokenness and messiness was strewn about like the toys of a toddler. Dad was completely and utterly exposed. There was no manufacturing; there was no social media projecting. Dad was who he was in raw form. He was exposed, but would he also be exposed to himself?

The artist Plumb in her song, "Lord, I'm Ready Now," does not laud being exposed as if it is good in and of itself. Instead, being exposed can have a positive outcome because it results in beauty. Being exposed is always a thing of beauty by virtue of who emerges: the inner self.[1]

Being exposed is another way of saying that you're being freed from current life, which is hiding the true life that is within you.

Being exposed ends the cycle of projecting the ideal you've presented to the world. Being exposed strips off the mask.

Dad, by virtue of being exposed, emerged as someone that is beautiful too. In his weakness and brokenness, the inner man who long hid behind a manufactured existence finally surfaced. And he was beautiful.

Dad's beauty—his sensitive, honest, confessional self—was a surprise to us all. I think it was even more of a surprise to Dad. Several times in our conversations, he would pause, mid-sentence, somewhat shocked at what he was saying and somewhat trying to encourage his own bravery. Only once did he acknowledge his surprise. It was short yet explicit: "I don't usually talk like this, Ryan."

I knew that, and he knew that I knew that.

"This is unusual of me," he said, "and I need to openly acknowledge that so as to palliate my nerves." I think he was surprised at his own vulnerability, his own exposure. He was learning in those final days that there was more than the image he had projected and believed about himself. I just smiled, pretty sure that Dad needed to convince himself it was okay to be hosting this much, to be so exposed. Inside, I was cheering on his bravery.

My aunt Shirley knew my father had a beautiful inner self locked safely away from others. "I wish his true self would come out from behind that anger," she told me over the phone a few weeks before my visit. Her wish was clairvoyant in that my father's true self was finally emerging.

Through hosting us all, a man who was guarded and stoic, finally cracked open. Like a fearless child, not yet bruised and hardened by the pounding of life, Dad shared feelings and his tears, and most importantly, he learned to be honest with himself.

As we sat there and chatted, I was sensing it was time to give Dad a break. Something gnawed at me, like a small dog tugging at my pant leg. More annoying than painful, my heart kept saying: *It's time, it's time, it's time.*

Tucked away and hidden was the forgiveness I wanted to give Dad. He deserved my forgiveness in that he stood before me naked, human, scared, and apologetic. He was not the only benefactor. I was also, even more so. He deserved forgiveness, but I *needed* it.

For some time, I have believed that to withhold forgiveness is to remain in bondage. Dad's love was loosening the fetters around my wrists, the muzzle on my mouth, and encouraging me forward. But my fear convinced me that the timing was critical. I argued with my heart: *Timing is everything,* I told myself.

Timing is another word for strategy. It's cold. It's corporate. Timing is fundamentally about controlling environments, or at least capitalizing on the ideal environmental conditions. Timing is about prediction. To use a more corporate term, timing is about *forecasting.* Concern for timing is about avoiding risk and vulnerability. While timing makes sense in a board meeting, it fundamentally removes the humanness out of an encounter with another.

Voltaire said that we are all full of errors, so we should forgive each other our follies.[2] In my time with Dad, I had come face to face with a man who was suffering but willing to love. He was deteriorating but capable of the energy to take risks. Everything

138

from his confessions to his fears was a type of self-emptying. He was vulnerable. He was sharing his errors. Timing *wasn't* a concern.

I sat, slightly elevated in comparison to Dad's slouch, my ego intact, waiting for good timing. Then it became clear: my error, my risk, was not at all of the same nature as Dad's. My error was in the very act of withholding forgiveness until the timing was right. I was trying to maintain control. While Dad revealed his errors by being vulnerable, I was withholding vulnerability itself.

I mustered up the courage like a child before jumping off the diving board for the first time. I mentally climbed the ladder, walked to the end of the diving board, put my toes over the edge, and gave myself a pep talk. *You can do this, Ryan. Just tell him. It'll be freeing. You can do it. One, two, three . . .*

"Dad, I want you to know something."

I looked down at the floor, the natural gaze of one cowering.

Ryan, look at him. You owe it to yourself to look at him and tell him how you have processed through his failures as your father. Look at him.

I looked up, my innards in my throat, and managed to eke out, "I forgive you, Dad. I don't harbor any resentment. In me there is only forgiveness."

What was held in for thirty years came out in ten world-altering seconds. I could feel the magnitude of the moment in my nerves. My fingers tingled, and my senses heightened. I saw patterns in the golden grass through the window nearest Dad's chair. I could hear the ticking of the second hand on the clock behind my left ear. I could smell the cinnamon candle on the end table. My flight or fight responses were fully engaged.

I jumped up and started straightening the room, avoiding the fact that I'd released myself from the prison of resentment. It was a supreme risk, with a lot at stake, and there I was fluffing pillows.

After a moment, I blurted, "So . . . um . . . you think teaching might be an option for me?"

I can't believe I said that! It was meaningless, a last ditch effort to hide and not talk about the elephant in the room. Looking back, I question why I was trying to hide at all.

The reality was that I was terrified of becoming truly equals. Through forgiving Dad, I was taking a monumental risk. We became risk-taking equals. I had been present with Dad, sincerely and genuinely connecting, for many hours. He trusted me and invited me further into his weakness. But the dynamic was imbalanced. He was weak; I was strong. He was sick; I was healthy. He was the host; I was the visitor. While I had left religious platitudes and evangelistic pushiness behind, I still held onto the paramount difference between us: Dad had taken a bigger risk than I had, and he was more vulnerable and exposed.

Extending the forgiveness balanced the scale and made us equals. And it was terrifying. We were both now truly standing together in mutuality. I knew it and I think Dad did too.

"Ryan," he said, "all I can think about is you forgiving me. That was so important to me. It's all I can think about right now." This was his way of relieving my fears.

I'M GOING to lean on Emmanuel Levinas here again, like I did in the last chapter. He says if you are truly listening to someone, you don't take note of the color of their eyes.[3] The objective details of the other are but a blurry backdrop to the genuine experience of subjectivity. We might say that in truly listening, the other is not a transmitter of information as much as he or she is a contributor to the relational dynamic. While listening names the act of hearing words, it's more about entering a mutual space and blurring the distinctions between two subjects.

The experience of "getting lost" in another's story captures the kind of listening I'm talking about here. The other is no longer a distinct object capable of being experienced or analyzed as separate. Instead, the other is part of a subjective, human connection.[4]

I found Levinas's point to be true with Dad. His clothes, his piercing blue eyes, even the room and its surroundings all faded away. All that came into focus was one who was wounded. In the moment that I reciprocated Dad's risk with my own risk, we were mutuals. There wasn't the suffering and the visitor; we were both fallible, full of error, full of monsters and ghosts, facing each other in love.

In the blemishes on his tired skin were my very own scars. In his famished body were my own wounds. Wounds are "stories" written on one's body. They are to be heard and held and ultimately entered. The stories we tell and the ones our bodies tell are invitations to mutuality.

Like a football player who bears witness to the brutality of the sport through his body, the stranger on the Emmaus Road had this witness. Crucifixion is brutal. The victim is beaten. Bones break. Joints pop. The stranger bore scars in his wrists and on his feet and in his flesh. By physically approaching the men on the road, the stranger's wounds were fully exposed.

Cleopas and his brother reciprocated the risk with an invitation. The invitation was an affirmation of the stranger's wounds, not by pointing them out and thereby making them a spectacle, but rather by bearing witness to their own painful lives. In other words, by way of invitation they became mutuals.

I experienced this with Dad.

We both took risks, our wounds were affirmed, and we were mutuals.

ONE OF THE many symptoms of ALS is difficulty with breathing and swallowing. Because the disease attacks the neurons in the brain associated with moving muscles, it is not uncommon that the muscular demands of a patient's throat and lungs are compromised.

By Friday evening, my father's breaths were short and forced. His supplemental oxygen tank sat behind his chair in the corner of the living room, out of sight. From the kitchen, Mom noticed Dad's struggles and offered him help. When he gave a thumbs-up, I jumped off the couch and grabbed the tank. I handed Mom the nasal cannula, which looked like a large tangle of clear plastic tubes. She surveyed the tubes for a few moments, confidently tugged them loose, looped them around my father's ears, and inserted the two prongs into his nostrils.

Seconds after she turned the oxygen tank on, an immense relief came over him. Dad's alertness spiked. For the first time in weeks his lungs didn't labor for oxygen.

He surprised us both when he asked for some of the clam chowder he smelled simmering in the kitchen. Along with the loss of strength to his lungs, the swallowing experience was atrocious. Eating was a tightrope walk between going hungry and asphyxiation. Evidently, the oxygen was a gift of energy and a gift of confidence. Dad requested a bowlful of soup and he devoured it. Before I finished mine, he was asleep.

I finished my soup, then headed into the kitchen where Mom was still in shock from the effects the oxygen had on Dad's energy and appetite, and gave her a long hug. I told her to call me if he woke up, that I was going to spend the evening getting fresh air and processing all that had happened.

I left Dad's side that evening believing that the most beautiful things in life are not fully understood intellectually but are nonetheless fully and passionately lived despite certainty. Life is too messy and unpredictable. To live faithfully is to follow a Divine call forward into this world *without* systematic understanding, and yet still with the faith to fully engage the messy unknown.

For me being faithful meant being vulnerable and getting messy. Thursday and Friday with my father didn't go as planned; it didn't end as planned either. However, in the midst of the messiness, there was redemption.

Redemption is a theological term that refers to the deliverance from sin and bondage (from the Latin *redemptio,* to buy back, release, or ransom). While redemption specifically refers to the saving significance of the death of Christ,[5] it also includes the more broad meaning of release from captivity.[6] In other words, redemption is not only a reference to what was "spiritually" achieved through the crucifixion; instead, it refers to a very concrete liberation and experience of freedom.

But it is not a freedom *from* the messiness of life; rather, it is a freedom *within* the messy uncertainties and absurdities of life. In this way, redemption is not freedom from the universal experience of trauma, but instead, it actually empowers us to face the trauma so that it loses universal control over us. Redemption is not the freedom from the crucifixion, but a disarming of the power of the ugliness and trauma of the crucifixion.

I believe redemption names the call of God to not run away but toward and into this very real and messy life. Redemption is the freedom we experience when we are able to face the inevitable trauma head on. Only then does the beauty within the mess emerge.

Friday was messy and ended with unpredictable abruptness, but Dad and I followed the call to emotionally connect as mutuals. The bondage of emotional distance was broken. For the first time, we confessed and shared forgiveness. The bondage of unreconciled hurts was broken.

The power of my father's crucifixion was weakened.

We experienced redemption.

V

HOPE RETURNS

When he was at the table with them,
he took bread, gave thanks,
broke it and began to give it to them.
Then their eyes were opened and they recognized
him.

— LUKE 24:30–31

16

SLUMBER

A FAMILY'S DOMESTIC CULTURE IS A COMBINATION OF VALUES AND norms. Values are the subjective beliefs that help constitute what's good and bad. Norms are the means of fulfilling family values through habits, practices, and traditions. Values are the beliefs; norms are the practice of beliefs.

The specific way to perform certain practices is an issue of etiquette, which might be defined as the unwritten code of behavior in a domestic culture. Values are the beliefs, norms are the practices, and etiquette is the way the practices are performed.

There is a pronounced Fasani family culture, and though unwritten, certain behavioral etiquette is very clear. One defining value is male masculinity, which is no surprise in a family of five boys. The norm is to stay physically fit, establish patriarchal leadership in the home, and be the primary breadwinner. There is a proper etiquette in performing these norms, of course. Certain clothes are acceptable, certain verbiage is encouraged, and certain attitudinal dispositions warranted.

An explicit etiquette—as vivid in my childhood memories as it is powerful in the present—is the proper display of emotions. Our family culture required a type of emotional stoicism. In childhood, crying was a sign of weakness and complaining was forbidden. Emotional fortitude was lauded.

The deep slumber that was welcomed Friday evening became Saturday morning's terror. Dad didn't wake up.

Rob, Rocky, and I immediately went to my parents' house after Mom texted us about Dad's status. Dad hadn't slept well in a year, so a deep sleep was quite a blessing. But sleep that is too deep is frightfully similar to final rest. We were caught between a sense of relief and fear, a nowhere land of emotions. Rocky attempted to gently wake Dad but with no success. Rob and I walked in circles, stirring the ingredients that went into this unexpected morning, trying to make something of it that was palatable. It wasn't working. We were lost, confused, and worried this might be the end. Randy was only five minutes away, but Rick was an hour away.

When Randy arrived, there was a mild sense of relief knowing that we were one brother closer to all being together should Dad pass shortly. Randy walked in, nodded to acknowledge us all, and headed straight to Dad's chair.

There are different types of gaits, all with different purposes. A saunter, for example, is for sightseeing or daydreaming; to skulk is to walk without notice. Randy's walk was decisive and confident. He *strode* to the corner of the room where Dad was sleeping and sat down. He didn't bend at the hip in a type of bow, lowering his head with respect. He didn't kneel on one knee to be at Dad's eye level. He sat on the floor. There was commitment to his sitting, a resolution that this moment warranted a different posture. From the nod to the stride to the sitting, I knew something was about to decisively change.

Randy, the biggest of all five sons, had chosen the lowest of positions. He sat at the base of the chair, holding Dad's leg. He began to cry. Any inhibitions he might have had were left outside. His walk said he had business to tend to: the business of weeping. He cried for almost twenty minutes. Randy, a prototype of masculinity—six-four, muscular, a commanding physique—sat broken open and grieving.

What changed at that moment was not the state of Dad's body or the stage of Dad's death. In some ways it was more poignant, more impactful. What changed was that grown men could now wail. Grown men could fall to Dad's feet, hold his leg, and let snot and tears pour forth. We could now fully feel and fully be present in the pain and turmoil of Dad's imminent death. Randy boldly broke etiquette.

Breaking etiquette is like breaking a window. Unfamiliar elements are free to come in. What's outside is unpredictable and wild. When etiquette is broken, it's not the infraction itself that scares us the most. What's scarier is that the unfamiliar "out there" may come rushing in. But an even bigger fear is that the unfamiliar "out there" may reveal the absurdity of "in here." The threat is that we will see in plain sight that our norms are not normal everywhere. Perhaps more straightforward, breaking the etiquette of culture runs the risk of allowing the fresh air of change to waft in.

Jesus broke etiquette while he was sitting at the table with Cleopas's family. When he picked up the bread and began to lead the meal, any smidgen of predictability they might have had was lost. A loss of control hovered ever so close to the table, as everyone was on edge, expecting the worst.

It was necessary for Jesus to break etiquette to release Cleopas and his family from the restrictions on their imaginations. It shattered the old, making way for the new. There was a new Kingdom, a new ruler, a new future. The old, including the norms and etiquettes of family life, was being reshaped and re-envisioned. Breaking etiquette prepared their eyes to see that the new Kingdom stood in contrast to the old, and the normative ways of life must be changed.

Randy's decision to sit and cry cracked the window of etiquette Saturday morning. The more he cried, the more it splintered, eventually shattering. Fresh air blew in, and fresh practices rushed in. Randy's action made way for all five brothers to feel with raw, uninhibited emotions.

The shattering of etiquette offered the option to be broken with Dad's brokenness, to suffer with Dad's suffering, to fully feel the experience of Dad's imminent death. The tears and snot were a type of lubrication for new behavior, which authorized five grown men to really weep with our father.

Dad was breathing but not responsive. Several times I tried waking him. I held his hand. "Dad can you wake up? We're here."

It didn't work.

I held his hand and his elbow and shook as I said, "Dad, didn't you want to talk and ask questions?"

One hand on his arm and one on his knee now. "Dad, are we going to walk together?"

Only a grunt in response.

I wanted to honor his request to walk together to the end. When he made that request, I didn't imagine him eating a bowl of soup and falling asleep, never to wake up. That wasn't how it was supposed to end! I pictured Mom and me on either side of him, Dad asking questions, me enjoying the intimacy, and Mom in an end-of-life sort of trance. I pictured Dad engaging in a rich dialogue that faded into blissful rest.

That wasn't how it was unfolding. What I expected was not being fulfilled. What I was *certain* would happen was not happening.

Certainty is not a characteristic of the process of dying. There are too many unknowns. Being this close to someone who was dying reminded me that the trajectory of life is always a process of dying. The finality of life may be near or far, but dying is always underway. Life, as it were, is a slow death.

This is why certainty is not a luxury in life either. This may be cause for resistance; it might trigger a defense of absolute truth or an apology for having confidence in one's faith. I think it should cause the opposite. Instead of uncertainty and unknowing being a threat to faith, which is an expression of the fundamental belief in the Divine, they should strengthen faith.

Consider Jesus before his identity was revealed at the table in Cleopas's house. He bore on his body the scars of torture and its aftermath (death). Regardless of cause, death is a sea of questions. How fast will it happen? Will it hurt? How will I know it's upon me? What happens the moment it's over? Only days earlier, Jesus was asking questions in the throes of his own dying. "My God, my God, why have you forsaken me" (Matt 27:46)? He experienced a combination of abandonment and unknowing at the scene of his own death. One could say that at the supreme moment of Jesus' faithfulness, he was flooded with doubt. (This alone is solace in doubt and uncertainty!)

Working backwards, Jesus foresaw the immanence of his death during the Passover celebration in Jerusalem. He gathered his closest apprentices and explained the trauma that would unfold. From there, they visited their favorite prayer garden so Jesus could grieve the coming torture. Relative to most, Jesus knew a lot about his death before it happened. But even with the advantage of knowing, his confidence was waning. "Please take this cup [of suffering] from me" (Mark 14:36). In other words, even with the facts of his death in hand, the experience of death and dying is replete with fear and uncertainty. Knowing the details does not strip death of its inherent unknowing. Even with omniscient insight into his own death, Jesus still experienced uncertainty.

But he was faith-full. And that is possible because certainty and faith are not synonyms. In times of death, they are at odds. Theologian Paul Tillich is often given credit for saying that the opposite of faith is not doubt, it's certainty.[1] What Tillich means is that faith requires complete surrender by the one who holds to its claims. And by surrendering—even surrendering certainty itself—one is open to ultimate meaning.

While certainty purports to inhibit confusion and incredulity, it also resists surprise, revelation, and wonder. Certainty protects, while doubt explores. Certainty withdraws and stabilizes, while doubt and unknowing investigate and search. Faith is not certainty in the face of death; faith is the embracing of uncertainty, that we might be surprised by revelation and taken in by the wonder and beauty that emerge. If embraced, the uncertainty within the experience of death opens us to receiving meaning—lasting, deep, substantive meaning—rather than answers.

Before his own death, Plato famously advised his students to practice dying while they lived.[2] Perhaps the wisdom here is that dying is not only an end-of-life experience but is an integral part of the process of truly living. Are we not all dying slowly?

If so, then uncertainty and unknowing are inherent components of living. This should not cause concern for the religiously faithful. Instead, it should intensify our openness to being surprised by the One to whom we are faithful. Doubt and uncertainty should be embraced and harnessed so that we might have a richer faith marked by surprise, awe, and wonder.

Religious certainty is a type of fortress we build to protect ourselves from difficult questions and doubts. *Fortress* in this context is an impenetrable castle—it's built with apologetic walls to safely seal out the threat of questions and doubt.

There are three major problems with the defensiveness implicit in religious certainty. First, the fortress of certainty traps us inside, inhibiting us from the daring nature of faith. Faith dares us to learn, explore, and understand. It's not static but dynamic. When faith loses risk, it falls flat. But faith clamors to get out and be alive. Faith wants us to escape the confines of a fortress, to explore the breadth and beauty of creation, but also the depth and darkness of human experience.

Second, doubt and unknowing already exists behind the walls. Because we try to deny and suppress our doubt, it erodes the very foundation of our fortress. Faith is not secure in its own false protection but in the protection that comes only from freely, boldly, and honestly exploring the depths of our unknowing and fears. Doubts are only a threat to faith insofar as they are denied, villainized, and suppressed. Building walls temporarily protects faith, but in time, the inevitability of unknowing will cause the walls to collapse.

Third, there may be a perception that there's a threat of an attack, but the threat is only perceived. It's a projection of doubt, which we try to cope with by using control and certainty. That pseudo-certainty takes the form of a defense wall. A truly secure faith is not defensive but open to new understanding and further meaning. A fortified faith can't be threatened.

I realized that waking Dad up was like building a fortress. I feared not knowing, being out of control. What other questions might he have? Where was he in terms of his fears of dying? What was the state of his spirit in relationship to the eternal future? I thought I needed to know. What I actually needed was to acknowledge the gift that is *not* knowing. The gift is being uncertain yet present, unsure but close. What I needed was to embrace uncertainty and to have "more" faith.

After taking a fifteen-minute break, I grabbed my father's hands in mine, but this time through tears, I said, "Dad, wake up so we can finish our talk. Dad! Dad! Can you hear me?"

He just barely cracked open his eyes and grunted.

I laid his hand gently back down and walked away with a sense of defeat. I walked to the kitchen. I stared out the window. I breathed deeply. I was exhausted.

The two disciples were full of questions. Their journey from Jerusalem, the site of the crucifixion, to Emmaus, a reminder of failure and lost hope, was full of uncertainty and doubt. Their conversation with the stranger began with a question. And surely their guest's breaking of etiquette raised some more. Their lives as apprentices of Jesus abruptly ended, the redemption of Israel was over, and their Messiah was dead—all three experiences were a type of dying. In all that dying and loss, the disciples were utterly confused. They had no answers, only doubts.

But their thorough sense of unknowing provided the necessary condition for them both to be surprised by the revelation of Jesus' identity in their home. Cleopas and his brother could not deny their uncertainty, which made room for the novel, the new, the surprise.

It dawned on me that while I was wrestling with uncertainty, perhaps Dad wasn't. Maybe I was defending against doubt while he embraced the very presence of it. I asked myself, *Could I be the one without faith, veiling its lack with a concern for certainty?* I sat with that difficult question.

And then many more equally challenging questions came to mind. Were Dad's concerns satisfied and his questions answered in the very process of owning his weakness, his uncertainty, and his unknowing? Perhaps Dad had already met the conditions for being surprised by God. Did my father experience the surprising gifts of God through his confessions, my forgiveness, and our redemption? Does rest peacefully set in when we no longer need to work so hard to uphold certainty, justify ourselves in belief, or argue for absolutes? When the walls of certainty are allowed to crumble, does it look like my father's deep slumber?

Maybe it wasn't the bowl of clam chowder. Maybe it wasn't supplemental oxygen. Or perhaps it wasn't *only* those two things that ushered Dad into a deep slumber. Maybe Dad was faith-full and he rested at peace in his faithfulness.

I, on the other hand, was facing my fortress, and I was exhausted.

17

I LOVE YOU

MY FATHER WAS STILL BREATHING AND CALMLY RECLINING IN HIS blue chair in the corner of the living room. But the inconspicuous truth still hung like a marquee, flashing lights on the wall: Death is near. I accepted that his unresponsiveness was likely permanent.

Rick arrived to the house and all five brothers were together. My mother huddled us in the kitchen and proposed that we call hospice. We agreed that was the right next step, and within minutes a team of nurses were at the front door. We were no longer locked into the misnomer that grief and darkness be avoided, as if they steal our joy or weaken our spirits. Dad's exposure and Randy's freedom became the guide that held our hands, walking us toward loss with expectancy and hope.

With gentleness and respect, nurses moved efficiently around Dad's chair in the living room. In moments, the blue leather recliner was removed and my father was lying on a medical bed. He appeared so much more comfortable in that bed, but it was yet another symbol of how close we were to the end.

There's a quote in Henri Nouwen's book, *The Dance of Life,* that came to me on a sticky note from a friend. Nouwen says, "True joy often is hidden in the midst of sorrow, and that the dance of life finds its beginnings in grief."[1] We grabbed Dad's hands and began to dance.

As I remember it, as soon as the nurses left, Rob danced first.

A son who never so much as gave a cordial hug or a handshake to Dad shucked his inhibition and recklessly shared his affection. Rob pulled a stool up to Dad's side. He held Dad's hand. With his free arm, Rob braced himself, his left elbow on his knee, holding up the weight of his torso. He was in a type of prayerful lean forward, his and my father's hand folded in front of his face. In a posture of prayer, Rob spoke words from the heart: "Dad, we're here, we're with you. We love you, Dad. I love you, Dad." He said many other things that I couldn't hear but appeared in the same spirit.

The cheek of a young son is where a father puts his hand, cupping the very face of his own kin in his palm to assure safety and to guarantee love. Rob created that touch. He took those hands—one his, one Dad's—and brought them to his cheek. That touch pronounced a truth: *this* son and *this* Dad are endeared, one to another. Any distance from childhood, any barrier of safety between two men dissolved at that moment.

Rick danced second.

Along the side of Dad's bed, he entered into a holy place with these words: "Dad, we love you. All your boys are here. You're safe, Dad." He held Dad's hand and leaned closer toward Dad's face. In his own way, Rick broke an intimacy barrier, once and for all.

The most sacred places—those that are indwelled with deep holiness—must be entered with equally deep reverence. If not, profound offense occurs, a sense of extreme threat. The sacred barrier between two faces only inches apart is like this, only to be crossed with sincere trust and reverence. No longer would Dad be distant physically and emotionally. Rick entered the space between himself and Dad—two faces reverently and intimately peering toward each other—and it was holy.

For hours Dad lay silent, and then he began a series of grunts. We all formed a crescent around his bed. Mom was holding Dad's legs at the end of the bed, Rick and Rob were on each side of the bed holding Dad's hands, I was standing near Mom's back, Randy was kneeling near Dad's shoulders, and Rocky stood at Dad's feet. My father was moving a lot, as one might that can't find a comfortable relationship with the mattress. He was moaning, fidgeting. Mom was anxious and tried to communicate: "Do you need something? Are you uncomfortable?"

His grunts escalated in volume, his squirms more pronounced. It seemed like this might be the moment right before his last breath.

Mom's anxiety turned to a mild hysteria. She raised her volume, "Mark, are you okay?"

Then there was a clear shift in her questions. She seemed to try to settle the fear that this was the end. "Jesus is Lord, isn't he? You're going to be okay. You can finally rest. You know we're here, right? We love you . . . you know that, I hope. You can let go. You don't have to fight anymore. We're going to see you in heaven, aren't we, Mark?"

Dad grunted in a kind of affirmation to each question, or at least in acknowledgment of the concern behind each question.

Then he lifted his head. The grunts and now the movement demanded everyone's attention. In a loud volume, Dad rattled, "I love you, I love you, I love you, I love you, I love you, I love you."

Dad was terse but the words were no less meaningful. With a tone that could only mean he was drawing from a deep feeling of love and gratitude, he pointedly told each of us what had been restrained for years. The spirit of those final words looked straight into the eyes of each son and spoke softly.

"I love you, Rick."

"I love you, Rob."

"I love you, Randy."

"I love you, Ryan."

"I love you, Rocky."

In his bed, he was wrapped in uninhibited love and he reciprocated that same love for each of us.

Hope broke into the room at that moment. Heaven filled our hearts while the tune of grief filled our ears. I can't help but believe that such hope began with the immanence of God in the face of grief. But equally so, our accepting of uncertainty, breaking etiquette, and embracing vulnerability were the conditions for hope to break in.

18

HOSPITALITY

THE BURN IN THE HEARTS OF THE DISCIPLES ON THE ROAD TO Emmaus could be described as a type of ineffable awareness, a Divine confirmation that is known but not understood. I have related it to the feeling the disciples likely felt when they first heard John the Baptizer preach in the countryside. Something deep within them served as a barometer of truth, an existential trigger for purpose. There was more to the disciples' invitation than a penchant to host. There was more to their insistence than mere risk. These two men were moved on their walk, and they were motivated by that same anatomical burn to invite the stranger to stay. Was the warmth they felt a form of love reemerging in their hearts, not knowing it was the Jesus they loved only days before?

Hospitality is different from hosting. Hosting happens when we open our front door and welcome the other into our private domain. The life we live is in jeopardy of being exposed as different from the inner life of who we really are. This is the reason it's so risky. Hosting acknowledges that risk and welcomes the guest despite it.

Hospitality, however, goes further. It not only acknowledges that risk but *embraces it through love.* In the New Testament, hospitality (Greek: *phileo,* love; *xenos,* stranger) literally means "to love a stranger." Whereas hosting runs the risk of exposure, hospitality is a willing exposure over time. My true self is always exposed through the risk taking inherent in love.

As the one who is offering hospitality, I'm embracing the fact that my life is not always a perfect reflection of who I am. Loving the other requires an awareness of the fraud that I am in advance of the encounter, which is to say, to love another, I first must love myself despite the ugly truths that are within. Is not love first a love of oneself? That is why the greatest commandment—"Love your neighbor as yourself" (Mark 12:31) —begins within. Hospitality implies this truth about love. Perhaps this is why it's so difficult.

The guest who receives my hospitality is always on some level a stranger because his life is always an inaccurate reflection of his inner self that I do not fully know. As the one offering hospitality and love, I do not fear that disparity but welcome it. Is not love the commitment to learning the truth about another over time? This is why hospitality is always a type of hosting, but hosting is not always hospitality. Hospitality is always a loving act—loving of self and loving of a stranger. I can host and remain detached, even cold. That's not hospitality. Hospitality always engages in love.

The disciples wanted to do more than merely unlatch their front door and host the fellow traveler. The warmth in their hearts was being extended to the talkative stranger in the form of hospitality. They were extending the generous hand of love without knowing Jesus' real identity. They were committing, as love does, to continue learning the truth about who he was.

Because hospitality is extending love to a stranger, it is fundamentally an affirmation of his personhood. The stranger's value precedes his identity; his value is affirmed *before* he is fully disclosed. Hospitality always makes the claim that one's value is not contingent on any other factors than the fact that he exists. Beyond personality, appearance, wealth, prestige, and identity is a person of inherent value and worthy of love. Hospitality says, "By virtue of being an other, you are welcomed and valued in my presence."

The rumors of resurrection suggest a reversal of the death of Jesus. Resurrection is not, however, the antithesis to the crucifixion. It is maybe its undoing, but it's not its opposite. Instead, hospitality is the antithesis to crucifixion. It's a type of counter-crucifixion. An understanding of the effects of crucifixion help support this.

Crucifixion is not mere killing; it is calculated subtraction. The sufferer is removed from all social, political, and religious inclusion. It is a supreme form of isolation. The crucified is literally subtracted from his own existence, removed from his own identity. Crucifixion is a definitive "no" to one's value, which is why the crucified is considered cursed even by God. Hospitality is a definitive "yes" to one's value, an inclusion into relationship. To be welcomed despite disclosing one's true self or past actions is considered a Divine blessing. It's a blessing beyond merit, given out of love.

The Emmaus story helps us see that we need to practice radical hospitality. To do so, we need to resist the political powers that institute crucifixion, to revolt against torture and unnecessary death, to oppose inhumane alienation and isolation, and ultimately to subvert an ideology that justifies such injustices. Through loving strangers, we welcome, value, and affirm the other. Through loving strangers, we upend suffering and isolation. The disciples' hearts burned with the power to resist crucifixion by welcoming and loving the yet-to-be-revealed stranger on the road.

In many ways, Dad was a stranger. He spent many more hours in his home office disengaged than he did in the living room or the kitchen engaging with us. Though he formally fulfilled his obligations to us as a father, he was distant. He paid bills but rarely paid attention. He provided a roof and room but seldom provided a hug and an embrace. He was also dying and suffering from a type of crucifixion. ALS alienates, tortures, and subtracts the victim from all things that are familiar, and Dad was suffering from all of these symptoms.

Dad was a crucified stranger.

So was Jesus.

Crucifixion is a means of dealing with the stranger's actions, not the stranger himself. One is convicted for what he has done not who he is. As a judicial tool, crucifixion ignores the person that is yet revealed and instead incriminates a static identity associated with an action. It is not loving. Love patiently awaits a person's true self to emerge over time, and love is open to being surprised by the emergence of a more beautiful, more endearing other.

We had a choice: we could perpetuate the crucifixion Dad was suffering, which would reinforce estrangement, or we could refute the crucifixion through hospitality. Crucifixion or its opposite? The former required nothing of us; the latter required our love. We chose hospitality, the definitive "yes" to Dad's value, an invitation into relationship. Our love covered up a multitude of sins (I Peter 4:8).

Not symbolically, not esoterically, but concretely—with tangible ramifications—Dad was experiencing a Divine gift. That gift was the gift of new identity. Though stricken to bed and inhabiting an unfamiliar, atrophied body, Dad became a beloved guest. He was the antithesis to a crucified criminal.

Hospitality has a spirit to it, and it is therefore a disposition as much as it is an invitation. This is why hospitality is not limited to the act of welcoming someone into our private space. Hospitality is also an extension of who we are in the shared space that is between us. The spirit of hospitality is the spirit of affirmation and welcome that exudes from us, thereby transforming space into something tangibly life-giving.

To extend a spirit of hospitality, I must first understand myself as a stranger. I am always discovering the depths of truth about myself that were previously a mystery. The first step to having a hospitable disposition is to love myself despite my own ignorance about who I am. To run from my true inner self resists the spirit of hospitality. This is why xenophobia (Greek: *xenos,* stranger; *phobia,* fear), which literally means "fear of the stranger," begins with the fear of the stranger within, the fear of the unknown person that is me.

Resisting the crucifixion from which Dad was suffering required a transformation of space. As long as his home was a domestic hospital room, the torturous power of ALS would prevail. If the bed and the room and the house were transformed into a space of loving acceptance, the spirit of hospitality could prevail.

But in order to extend loving acceptance, my brothers and I had to first welcome ourselves into that space. Our physical presence did not accomplish this. In our own unique way, we each had to accept and welcome ourselves as strangers in a strange land. We needed to extend hospitality to ourselves in our own frailty.

It seemed that we all showed up on that Saturday with unfinished business. We came with negative memories, regrets, hurts, and wounds that we hadn't reconciled. We bore in us the weight of wishing we had spent more time with Dad throughout the years. We were restless because of these burdens, and we struggled with the effects of suppressing them. We all arrived with incomplete work and incomplete emotions.

We were also ignorant. We had no explanations for what was happening or how events would transpire. None of us knew how to be a son to a dying father or a brother to a sibling with a dying father.

Death has a way of revealing the interpersonal work that was shelved for later. At death, there is no later; later is now. Being hospitable to ourselves would mean embracing the weight of regret, the burden of unfinished work with Dad, and accepting our ignorance in the *now* that is death.

We were able to embrace our ignorance because we did *not* have dying figured out, we did *not* have the answers to the eternal that was butting up against the present, and we were *not* scripted in our speech. We embraced our weaknesses and cried like wounded children incapable of resolving all the burdens and hurts. No pretending, no facades. No platitudes, no pseudo-experts. We were open about our weaknesses so we could be fully attentive to Dad in the mess of dying.

The measurable space that is Dad's living room changed through the acceptance of our unstable selves. And then, and only then, we were able to genuinely extend the spirit of loving acceptance to Dad. Our ignorance and weakness and failures became a kind of collective strength. Paradoxically, that collective strength appeared (and felt) like supreme weakness, but it proved to be the transforming power of love and hospitality.

On that day, Dad's living room filled with the presence of God. Similarly, and quite literally, God's presence filled the room when Cleopas and his brother welcomed the unnamed stranger into their home.

Both houses transformed into sanctuaries.

19

CONSUMING HOPE

I GRABBED A STACK OF WATER CRACKERS FROM THE KITCHEN AND placed them on a plate. I filled a glass with wine. I made my way back to the living room.

Everyone sat still, though we were all internally wading through dense emotions. I used the top of a stool as a makeshift circular table. We encircled the room, all looking toward each other. Dad was in the center. Our hearts were full, our eyes were swollen, and none of us sure what was next.

I broke the silence. "A friend asked me what I hoped to do on this trip home. I said that I wanted to have meaningful conversations with my father. I wanted to connect. That has happened in a profound way over the last couple of days. I wanted to share the Eucharist with Dad because it's one thing I can be sure we theologically agree on."

Looking at the Eucharist elements, rehearsing my desire to share that meal with Dad, and accepting the fact that it would not happen built an emotional pressure held back by the thin retaining wall of self-composure. I reached forward and touched the cracker. At that very moment, the wall gave way.

I sobbed.

Between the tears and nose blowing, I explained that Dad asked me to walk with him to the end. I lamented that the Eucharist table would have been a wonderful "bridge" we could have walked over. I explained I was lamenting that lost opportunity. "The best alternative I could imagine would be to share it with the family, in Dad's presence," I said.

I began to rehearse the liturgy from I Corinthians 11: "I pass on to you what was given to me. On the night Jesus was betrayed, after giving thanks, he took the bread and broke it, saying, 'This is my body broken for you, take and eat in remembrance of me.'"

I passed the crackers around, and then gestured to Dad, who was but barely living. I said that Dad's body was broken, but life would come from it. New life would emerge. But unless we are honest with our own brokenness, we will not experience that life. If we want to be the kind of husbands and brothers we desire, we too must be broken for our wives and families. For it was in Dad's brokenness that he became stronger; for it was in his exposure and risk-taking that he became more fully the husband and father he was supposed to be.

I continued with the liturgy: "This is the cup of the new covenant, poured out for you and the sins of the world." I raised the glass of wine. It had been an hour since Dad moved or made any sound, but he began to grunt, as if to get our attention.

Rick quickly responded, "Dad, what is it? Do you want something? Water?"

Dad made a small grunt.

"Some bread?" Rick asked.

Another small grunt.

Rick searched, looking around in confusion. Then he asked, "Dad, you want some communion wine?"

Dad responded with a two-syllable grunt, "Uh-huh!"

Unsure on how to get wine into the mouth of one lying supine, Rick opted for the plastic-needle syringe left by hospice. He checked to make sure the syringe plunger made good contact with the barrel, and pulled it in and out twice. Then he submerged the needle into the glass of wine and filled it. The room was silent as we watched in disbelief.

Rick inserted the syringe between Dad's left cheek and gums and slowly administered the wine. I worried the wine would fill his mouth and dribble down his lower lip. Dad had constantly drooled for the better part of the day, but not a drop of wine was lost. As a symbol of his resolution to participate, Dad summoned all of his strength to hold in that wine, to consume the elements with us.

I was trying to make sense out of what just happened. "Uh . . . in my understanding, only one of the elements is required for communion to 'count.' We just shared, for the first time, Eucharist with Dad." A miracle had unfolded in front of us. In a way, the magnitude of what happened didn't register until the very words fumbled out. I said it again to convince myself, "We just shared Eucharist with Dad." I had to stop at that point.

Then in a type of benediction, I said, "We are to go and do this in remembrance of the one who broke on our behalf, who inspires us to find strength in the humility of broken bodies. Dad's body is broken, and Dad reminds us that there is strength in vulnerability and weakness."

If hospitality is counter-crucifixion—standing in opposition to the devaluing of one's very personhood and his isolation from others—the Eucharist serves as the quintessential act of hospitality.

Eucharist is quite simply the invitation to the table that is set for Passover to remember the Exodus, the table Jesus hosted in the Upper Room, the banquet table of God. As such, what Eucharist *cannot* do is isolate individuals. The table meal is fundamentally communal, which is one of the reasons it is also known as communion. There will always be a host and a guest. It is not fast food; it cannot be taken to-go or eaten privately in the car. It happens at a table in the company of others. Isolation and Eucharist cannot coexist!

Because we name the table, the "Table of Our Lord," and we have stories to remind us from where the table came, we are prompted to receive the names of those who dine there and the stories from where they came. That's why anonymous eating cannot be done with the Eucharist. The table is named and narrated. The guests will not remain nameless strangers without stories. Crucifixion, torture, but also just the isolating hardships of life, strip people of their names and identity. The Eucharist returns and affirms those names and honors those stories.

The Eucharist conflates the infinite with the finite, the supernatural with food, and the Divine with bread and wine. While it sounds crass, the fact that the Eucharist liturgy acknowledges the body and blood of Jesus in the bread and wine, a beautiful awareness manifests: the temporal is of sacred presence. The dichotomies that we so often assume—sacred/profane, divine/human, religious/secular—are confused at the Eucharist table. We could say that the disparate categories in our dualistic worldview "commune" together at the table.

The pure form of welcoming the stranger is not to stop at valuing them as an other, but to value the very presence of divinity in them, embracing their infinite value. They are not dis-spirited bodies with a penchant for consumption; instead, they are spirited others indwelled with the very presence of God. So to extend hospitality is to acknowledge the very presence of God in our midst. The Eucharist makes this explicit. We are reminded of God's very presence at the table and those who will eat from that table.

When Dad asked if I would walk with him to the end and requested not to be coerced, what I think he meant was something akin to the reality of the Eucharist table. In his request was a groaning for intimate connection, a longing for community.

As he approached death, Dad feared that his past would revisit and haunt him. From what I gathered, he didn't fear the proverbial review of one's sins upon the entrance of heaven. Instead, he feared the very consequence of his sins persisting up to (and possibly through) the moment of death. Specifically, Dad requested that I walk with him so he might not experience the isolation from which he suffered for so many years.

He also feared the coercive tendency of end-of-life crusaders, people who project their own anxieties about death and the afterlife. In requesting not to be coerced, Dad had in mind a particular kind of non-isolation: a community of dignity and respect.

Virtually hours from entering a permanent sleep, my father was able to request the Eucharist, because in those very elements, *all* of his requests were met. At the Eucharist table, there is no isolation; there is only a dignifying community where all stories are heard and valued. By joining us at the table, Dad was joining us in affirming that his desire for community was fulfilled in the very presence of God.

The disciples had been trained under this logic. They were aware of the divine presence in this world. Their rabbi and leader was the embodiment of the truth that God takes on flesh among us. When they invited the stranger on the road in for dinner and offered him a bed to rest upon, they were (ironically) inviting him into the presence of God. The invitation was also an (ironic) affirmation of the divine value of the stranger. They were about to learn that the affirmations were true in ways they hadn't expected.

Dad's journey was about to end.

For over a year, he and my mother suffered under the painful side effects of one prescription medication after another. They plodded through the bog of medical procedures to no avail. For Those tests and prescriptions were evidence that Dad was a patient with a disease as much as he was a research specimen with a mystery to solve. Every appointment, every measurement or scan or probe, every trip to the pharmacy, was torture for Dad.

Saturday was the day that we put an end to the suffering, the medicine, the research, the guessing. We conceded to the immanence of death but not its power to keep hope distant. While death was close, God was closer. Dad welcomed—we all welcomed!—the presence of the God that bends down, comes near, joins us as a guest at the Eucharist table, and ultimately becomes the host. Despite death, hope returned to stay.

After a year of swallowing pills to try to heal his body, Dad swallowed the wine that healed his soul. After a year of being probed, pricked, and stuck with medical implements, there was a holy irony in the syringe administering the lasting healing, divine hope. No medicine can stave off the symptoms of crucifixion, and no injection can return hope and affirmation to the isolated and dying. Unless, of course, that syringe is filled with the presence of the Holy.

Brother Lawrence, the seventeenth-century Carmelite monk, articulated back then what we learned at Dad's bedside. The mundane objects, tasks, and challenges of this world can become the intimate experience of the Infinite Other. Lawrence was a dishwasher. In the basin of soapy water, food-laden dishes, and the tedious task of combining the two, God could be experienced as present.[1]

In the moment of breaking bread and sharing wine with Dad— the mundane task of eating—the wine-filled syringe carried new meaning. It now meant that God was close enough to be consumed, becoming part of the very frailty of Dad, transforming his weakness into strength, transforming the syringe of death into a vessel of hope.

Hope explicitly returned Saturday morning!

VI

HOPE AND MYSTERY

*They recognized [Jesus],
and he disappeared
from their sight.*

— LUKE 24:31

2 0

REVELATION

AFTER WE SHARED EUCHARIST, WE HUDDLED AROUND DAD'S BED and prayed. I looked up at the pine-paneled ceiling and the recessed lights as if to gaze at the very presence of God in that room. "God, be close in this time, be present in this room. God, Dad has opened himself, confessed mistakes, been vulnerable. He has received the Eucharist and joined us in worship. Please accept these as offerings. Accept these from his heart and be near."

"Amen!" Mom said to close the prayer.

"Amen," everyone responded in unison.

I looked out the window and noticed the morning overcast had finally parted and the sun shined in. "Mom, look at that," I said.

"I just noticed that too." Her smile suggested a contentment underneath her tears and swollen eyes.

"It's as if the whole thing is orchestrated," I said. "I couldn't have written a script any better if I had tried."

"Just beautiful. Every detail is just beautiful," she commented as we hugged.

I added another closing, so as to include our short dialogue into our prayer. "God, thank you for the details, for your hand in these final days. Oh, God, how I pray it continues. Amen."

"Amen," she said in agreement.

When we pray, we are sometimes simply retelling what is already evident. In a way, it's to remind ourselves of what has happened and confirm their importance. This doesn't make our prayer less meaningful but instead gives it a level of intimacy in the same way that we retell cherished memories to those dearest to us. By retelling those memories, we reiterate the gifts of those experiences and thereby secure a sense of gratitude about them. This kind of prayer is a form of two-directional thanksgiving—a reminder of the gift while giving thanks to the Divine Giver. Because God was close and miraculously evident in the smallest details that Saturday morning, our prayer was an intimate reminder of how thankful we were for the return of hope.

But there's another profound aspect to the prayer that morning. It was a reminder that we had even more questions. Through the act of speaking our prayers, we speak aloud and therefore hear, sometimes for the first time, our feelings, desires, questions, and fears. Prayer affords us the ability to vocalize our deepest thoughts that we otherwise might not be able to articulate. Prayer has the potential to disclose who we really are to the Divine but also reveal who we are to ourselves.

Our post-Eucharist prayer was a retelling of what happened, but it also had hints of discomfort and unresolved questions. In his semi-consciousness, could Dad sense the same closeness of God that we could? Would God remain explicitly close to the end? Did Dad experience redemption or wholeness as had appeared?

It's not often read this way, but given the nature (a conversational tone) and posture (standing, eyes open) of our family prayer, there's no reason Cleopas and his brother's response to Jesus' disappearance was not a prayer: "Were not our hearts burning within us while he talked with us on the road and opened the Scriptures to us?" (v32). The disciples prayed the way we prayed as a family. They retold what had happened in a way that secured their gratitude, but at the same time it was an admission that they still had questions.

Thanksgiving and uncertainty were the two marks of our prayerful response to the mystery that was Dad's final moments, God's potent and powerful presence. Thanksgiving and uncertainty were also the disciples' immediate response to God's mysterious presence, and now, disappearance.

PERHAPS THE GREATEST evidence that Jesus was revealed to Cleopas and his brother was the physical response to what they saw. They were compelled at the revelation of the Messiah in their midst to run back to Jerusalem on a dangerous road to tell what they witnessed. Revelation is never primarily a "still and quiet voice" that whispers truth in our ear for our own private knowing. It's not fundamentally about knowing information as if God is heavenly knowledge waiting to descend into the minds of ignorant subjects.

Revelation is less about information and more about inspiration, less about elucidation and more about transformation.

The disciples' encounter with the stranger-revealed-as-Jesus resulted in a change. In the slightest encounter with the Divine, their circumstance, perception, and behavior changed. And it compelled them to run back to Jerusalem, a change in location. We can say that what begins in revelation will end in change. Their future would forever be different.

The change caused by revelation is not predictable, as if to follow a prescribed transition or a formulaic overhaul. Revelation describes an encounter with the in-breaking God, and it disorders that which we have worked hard to keep orderly. Breaking into our reality, our world, and our arena of existence, God disrupts our knowing, our expectations, our certainties. Revelation ruptures a present knowing while it informs and inspires new knowing. In other words, revelation makes a mess of what we know, which demands our attention and inspires a response.

While revelation is primarily about transformation, it is by definition a disclosure of Divine truth or insight. How can receiving Divine truth confuse us? How can more understanding disrupt what we know? Information gathered through revelation is not so much a list of facts as it is an enlightenment. Revelation is about knowing something new but also about changing the conditions of knowing altogether. It is about seeing more clearly and changing the conditions of seeing.

When God has been revealed, we do not carry more information of God around with us like an object of study.

Instead, God enables us to see and relate to all objects differently.

Because revelation disrupts knowing and enlightens understanding—the conditions for a new future—the revelatory moment for the disciples was when they shared Eucharist, not when Jesus' identity was revealed. In other words, seeing Jesus was the *result* of revelation. Through the disruptive, revelatory nature of the Eucharist, vision of everything changed. They now had the eyes to see (Matthew 13:16).

God was also revealed to Dad in the breaking of the communion bread. Like the disciples, Dad's response would suggest as much. At the disciples' table, nothing changed about the new host. What changed was the ability to see differently, more clearly, as the result of the revelatory bread breaking. Similarly, next to my father's bed, the broken and blessed bread became disruptive. Convalescing and barely conscious, it appeared that Dad was shaken awake by revelation.

The small plate, the broken bread, had become the site of revelation. Dad insisted on participating. It was a formidable response to the morsels of Divine disclosure around which we circled. The disciples were blind and then saw. They were closed and then opened to the image of the bent-down God in front of them. Dad was blind and then could see. Dad was closed and then opened.

We witnessed that enlightenment. We witnessed that transformation.

In his openness, my father was embraced by the Divine Host that presided at the Eucharist table. All five brothers were present, and we were more than spectators. We were participants in the revelation. We did more than merely observe the disruption of Dad's comatose state. Rather, we consumed the whole transformative experience, and every last crumb of the revelatory miracle unfolded in front of us.

My father had so many questions he needed answered. But revelation doesn't only disclose our true needs; it also changes the very conditions and experience of need. To those at his side on Saturday, it seemed my father's questions were answered in the very presence of God at the table. The Divine that was revealed through the bread *satisfied* his questions.

St. Augustine opens his *Confessions* reflecting on his own "restless heart" that could only find rest in God alone. The only place for satisfaction was in God alone.[1] Dad's heart was burning for final, fulfilling rest. Like Augustine and the disciples, I believe Dad found his fulfillment in the Divine Host of the Eucharist.

Our hearts were full too.

WHILE REVELATION RUPTURES what's normal, thereby eliciting a response, it is also mysterious. The revelation itself is not mysterious; rather, it reveals the infinite mystery of the Divine Other. In this way, revelation is a type of concealment.

Books were not fixtures in our home growing up, at least not in abundance. Mom read us children's books, but as we grew, we were responsible for our own reading. I'm assuming my father associated books with school and school with work. He either left his books in the classroom or hid them in his rectangular briefcase. My parents also preferred other reading than bound books: Dad read *National Geographic, Newsweek, Time*, and the local newspaper while Mom read the Sports section of the local paper.

There was one antique bookshelf. Its construction exuded a sense of integrity. There were four solid shelves, and each shelf had its own glass door that opened up and out like a garage door from the fifties. It was a beautiful piece of furniture. I remember two books that still call it home. The first was a medical resource book published by the Mayo Clinic—a colossal five-pound reference book that offered a bit of security to a mother with five rambunctious boys. The second was a four-hundred-page tome titled, *Evidence that Demands a Verdict* by Josh McDowell (and it was only Volume 1)! I paid this book a visit occasionally as a teenager when I needed quick answers to tough questions about the reliability of the Bible, evidence for the resurrection, or arguments for the existence of God.[2]

The brilliance of *Evidence* is how cogently the most complex religious and philosophical quandaries of human history are addressed. I remember as a teenager being amazed by the clarity with which McDowell and his eleven-person research team conveyed the truth. I envied not so much their ability to communicate, but the privilege they had of owning such a wealth of knowledge. If, by definition, revelation is the revealing or disclosing of information about God, then McDowell's team, by virtue of their breadth of knowing, must never have a doubt or question of uncertainty. I wanted that knowledge. I desired that certainty. I longed for that much revelation.

Having read some of *Evidence* during my visit with Dad, I realized that my teenage assumptions about the book were correct but the conclusions about the Divine were not. I assumed that arguments for the existence of God could be conclusively argued and thoroughly understood in four hundred pages. That assumption remains true, I believe. As a teen I concluded, as did the millions of other readers that devoured the "verdict," that the Divine is revealed clearly through concrete, revelatory "evidence." That conclusion proved to be untrue.

What I found so captivating as a teenager I found empty as an adult. My understanding of revelation has changed. My desire for certainty has waned. When I was young, I desired a God that was like a science experiment: observable, measurable, factual, provable. But in adulthood, specifically in the lurking presence of death, I "discovered" something different about revelation, about God. It challenged the conclusions I drew from *Evidence*.

Revelation elicits a response. It ruptures what's normal and transforms us. Also, revelation is always a type of *concealment* of the Divine. Paradoxically, what is revealed about the Divine always brings us closer to the *depth of the mystery*.

Mom and I had a moment of insight in our conversation Saturday, which helped me to better understand revelation. I was beginning to see revelation less like an answer to a math problem or the results of a science experience and more like encountering our beloved.

"Your father and I were planning to have so much fun. We just finished this stupid house. Dad didn't have to stress anymore," Mom commented.

"I know, Mom," I softly replied.

Dad had been asleep for almost twenty-four hours that Saturday afternoon. We were all exhausted from weeping. I put my arm around Mom, and we looked out the window toward the hills of grass and oak trees.

"This is not right. It's not fair. We were enjoying each other so much."

"I was blessed to see that," I affirmed.

"I was finally getting to know who he was . . . after all these years," she said through a flood of tears. "I was just getting to know him. He was being so nice to me."

"We could tell, Mom."

"We were gonna have so much fun," she insisted. "We were really enjoying each other's company. He was finally opening up. There was so much to discover in there."

I smiled—my heart smiled too—as any child does in the presence of loving parents.

Mom was expressing, among other things, a truth about love. Our understanding of our beloved does not end when we finally have them close—it just begins. We deceive ourselves when we believe that we would truly know the one we love if we could remove any distance between us. This is true on a basic level. We do know someone *better* the closer we get. But more deeply, when our beloved becomes close, we more fully encounter the mystery that is within them. The closer we become, the more we know how little we know.

Over the last year, my parents were falling in love. They were closer than ever before, and in my mother's words, "There was so much to discover." She was learning that the mystery was not in the man who was distant. Instead, the true mystery was in the heart of the man she was finally beginning to know when he was close. This mysterious depth, which can also be a mystery to the person himself, is an ever-expanding lure of our love and affection. It is never exhausted, only expanded.

Emmanuel Levinas said that the other is like a shore to which we will never arrive.[3] We set sail but never set our feet fully in the sand of our destination. In a truly loving relationship, one doesn't ever fully know the other, but instead only gets glimpses of just how much there is to still know. Only in closeness do we learn the depth of what we don't have of the other. Glimpses of the shore are all we have. They cultivate the desire for what we have but can't ever get enough of.

What about the Wholly Other, the Divine Other? God is an incoming God, breaking into our present reality. This is incarnation: the taking on of flesh and being revealed in the mundane realities of human existence. But the incarnation is the incoming of the Divine Mystery into our midst.

It is a mistake to think the Divine Mystery "out there" becomes the Divine Clarity "down here." The Divine Mystery "out there" *is now* the Divine Mystery "down here." In other words, while we learn a lot about the Divine through the incarnation, by virtue of proximity, the mystery is only confirmed in learning just how much we don't know. Like with our beloved, questions, curiosities, and our desire to know more only *increase* the closer the Divine comes.

Questions, not answers, are indicative of knowing and loving the Divine. Mystery, not "verdicts" that are demanded by "evidence," is indicative of knowing God.

The two disciples experienced this in a blink of an eye—the Divine presence in one moment, and the Divine disappearance the next. In that proximity—literally within reach, close enough to share bread—there was still an infinite distance. Jesus' disappearance was less a divine magic trick and more a confirmation of the nature of Divine revelation. The incarnation brings God close, but it also brings the Great Mystery within reach. This doesn't somehow demystify the Divine Mystery but instead makes known the expanse of our unknowing, which inspires, awes, and causes wonderment.

What my mother learned about my father during their falling in love was what the disciples learned about the incarnate God during his disappearing from their table: revelation is at once revealing and concealing, clarifying and mystifying.

Perhaps Dad's questions were a confirmation that he was experiencing the same closeness of the Divine that I was sensing. Perhaps Dad wanting to walk with me to the end was a type of invitation to participate—or at least notice—the beloved relationship budding between him and God.

God was close to Dad that Saturday, but God's presence was not abrupt. They walked together for a few days before God ultimately welcomed Dad to the divine banquet table. I witnessed the final encounter, and I was also blessed to participate in the journey.

Divine closeness, like revelation itself, is witnessed in two ways. It's seen in the growing desire to step further toward the mystery and the reaction to it. God's closeness has a qualitative and quantitative effect. The former is a lure into the life of God, which is marked by amazement. The latter is some measured action in the world.

For the disciples, the burn in their hearts was the draw toward God, and the immediate return to Jerusalem was the action that validated their encounter with God. Dad also reacted to God's closeness. He overtly requested consuming the Eucharist—the act of consuming God and consuming *with* God as a guest at the table. But was there a qualitative change in Dad's relationship to God's immanence? Is there a moment we can point to that stands as the definitive allure for Dad's soul?

Thomas Merton, the Trappist monk, theologian, and poet, said that God is the mystery found at the center of our innermost self.[4] There is a divine immanence in the heart of every individual. Should they journey inward, they will encounter the presence of God. Mystery surrounds every meaningful experience of the human heart, for the closer we get to the human heart, the closer we get to God.

Many of the biblical authors pointed toward the same truth. From the beginning of the scriptures, where God breathes divine air into the very center of humanity to enliven its soil-formed body (Genesis 2:7), to the Pauline promise that God is in us, and offering hope to the glorious end (Colossians 1:27), God is portrayed as being deep in the heart of humanity.

For Dad, there wasn't a point in his journey when he turned his gaze toward the mesmerizing presence of the Divine. Then again, there wasn't a moment like that for Cleopas and his brother either. Jesus was close to them for nearly seven miles as they walked their road of lost hope and shame. They arrived, shared greetings, washed up, set the table, continued talking, and began eating. There wasn't one moment when the presence of God definitively enchant them. The enchantment, the allure, the fascination for Dad, like the disciples, happened progressively over time.

Our center, our inner life that is often hidden *and* hidden from us, is not a given; it must be journeyed toward, reflected upon, and danced with. Thomas Merton calls it "contemplative prayer," some biblical authors call it "meditation," and still others call it "listening to the soul." Jesus did not intentionally disclose himself at the dinner table. Jesus, the Son of God, was being revealed all along the journey. And the closer the disciples attuned themselves to the burn in their hearts, the closer they came to the Divine Mystery that sat in front of them.

Dad was on a journey too. The three days prior to the table, he chiseled back the barricade that sheltered him from himself and from God's presence. The suffering *and* the conversations, the weakness *and* reflection, awakened him to what was inside: a hurting and hungry heart and a Divine host offering comfort and a meal.

Dad's request for the Eucharist was an affirmation of his experience. Dad discovered in his heart an awe at the revelation of God that had broken in. It seemed that he was in awe of the God that requested the tables to be turned. And he became the guest of the hospitable God.

21

(DIS)APPEARANCE

THE END WAS NEAR.

Dad's autumnal desire to purposefully connect and reconcile with his sons was complete. My autumnal desire to share in one eucharistic table experience with Dad had been fulfilled. Winter's cold breath was sending the message that death was due and finality would soon envelop my father's life and his body.

There's one component of Dad's imminent death that avoided my attention until late Saturday evening. All the physiological measurements of living would cease. At some point in the near future my father's breath would stop, his heart would not beat again, and the synapses in his brain would not fire. I was already grieving those tangible losses. But what I had yet to consider was the concrete ending of Dad's life as it is experienced by his presence. In other words, Dad would *leave* and never come back. He would never shake my hand again or worry about me rotating my tires. He would die shortly. But he would also be taken away, removed from our familial existence, never to be touched or seen or heard again.

Dad would not only die soon, which is an irreversible ending, but he would leave, which is a type of irreversible emptying. Dad would disappear from our lives in a similar way that Jesus disappeared from the house of the disciples (v31). One second he was there, and the next second he was gone. Only a void was left to vouch for his presence.

I was sitting at the dining room table, which is the elbow between the living room where Dad lay and the kitchen where my brothers were congregated. They were snacking and looking out the window at the field we ran through as children. Dad was alone, intentionally. We invited Bob to come by so they could have time together.

We used to joke and say that Bob Williams was Dad's only friend. It was funny, because it pointed at a truth that is rather difficult to talk about otherwise. Dad was hyper-reclusive, never once showing a genuine interest in social interaction. But it also points to another truth: to be Dad's friend required a particularly gifted person, one who could counter his cynicism with humor. Bob possessed this gift.

What began as an acquaintance at Rio Tierra Junior High School in 1971—Dad a reading teacher, Bob a physical education teacher—grew into a friendship over a shared interest in tennis and eventually developed into a formidable bond marked by humorous banter, political conversations, and marital commiseration. Bob had the uncanny gift of navigating Dad's negativity, ignoring his request for reclusion, and relentlessly pointing out Dad's idiosyncrasies. And he was hilarious. According to Mom, Bob was the only person who could make Dad laugh.

Bob stood on one side of Dad's bed, trying to find a comfortable distance. He judged the left side unsuitable, so he moved to the right side and made a considerable step closer to my father. Aside from his sons and wife, Dad would want Bob to pay him a visit at the end of his life. Bob was not a threat to my father's dignity. Bob reminded Dad that there's always at least one reason to smile despite the infinite reasons in this world to be upset and cynical.

I watched intently. I moved a bit closer to listen more carefully.

"Mark, I've never told you this before . . ." Bob managed to wrangle that first sentence out. He pulled out his handkerchief and blew his nose. He was crying. He took another small step forward and said, "You were such a good friend. I'm not sure what I'm going to do without you around," he said through tears.

Bob was communicating the depth of connection they shared. Their relationship was an intertwining, a fusion of being, one indistinguishable from the other. In a simple way, this happens by virtue of sharing experiences with a friend. Those experiences are at once individual but also communal—they will always be a memory of oneself *with* an other. "I'm not sure what I'm going to do without you around" captures this meaning. But it also captures how life tangles together over time between friends. A bond forms over memories, but also over shared interests, shared concerns, shared secrets, and shared loves, to name a few. Good friends are like tangled roots; they are inseparable and draw from the same source of nutrients. I think Bob meant it in both ways. They shared great memories; they also developed an inseparable bond.

Through his tears, Bob said, "Even though you always called me a jerk, I still love you."

Forty years of friendship and finally Bob could tell Dad how important he was. Four decades of talking over lunch breaks, competing in tennis, and sharing breakfast at the bakery off Douglas Boulevard, Bob was able to explicitly affirm their friendship and express his love.

Dad's death was opening up a new level of their relationship that was previously unexplored. In his departing, he was arriving to a connection that now included explicit affirmation and admission of need. In a way, Dad's leaving was a type of coming. Only now, in Dad's leaving and Bob's awareness of losing a friend, did they gain an awareness of the depth of their friendship, which was really a discovery of a previously unarticulated, mutual love. Only in Dad's imminent disappearance did he fully appear to Bob. Only in his absence were they fully and unreservedly present together.

***

JESUS DISAPPEARED, and like Bob, the disciples were present at the end. While his vanishing was a type of leaving, it was also an arrival. I can think of a few distinct ways that Jesus, at the moment of his mysterious and sudden departure from Cleopas' table, *fully arrived* in their midst. One way is an affirmation, another is an initiation, and yet another is a redefinition.

Jesus' disappearance was an *affirmation*. His leaving confirms the importance of loneliness—an affirmation of aloneness. One of the first questions a friend asks himself upon losing a companion is not where they are going or why they might have left, but instead is a question about himself: *What am I going to do without them?* Naturally, when we lose someone, we sense a profound loneliness. We are alone and grieving, full of questions and discomfort.

Jesus' disappearance exposes our aloneness to us, which is an abyss to be explored and understood. But who enjoys exploring deep, dark, and mysterious waters? No one. In the same way we don't enjoy exploring the deep abyss of our own self. But as Henri Nouwen says, these deep waters of loneliness are the sight of beauty, discovery, understanding, and vocation.[1] It's not God that relieves us from this discovery, offering a simple solution to our sense of loneliness. Only a false god would make this offer. God invites us to explore the treachery that is often the darkest crevasses of ourselves, for in them is endless learning and beauty.

From experience, it's in our loneliness that we discover the true meaning of our connections, and our need for and the nature of the love that seems to complete us. In the void, should we explore it, we discover the love from our past that was nurturing, and the love that was not loving at all. Until we're alone we cannot explore the textures of our loving connections, healthy or unhealthy. More importantly, in our loneliness, we discover the self-love that we've neglected to offer ourselves.

Another example from experience is the silence of being alone. In the silent separation from others, in the quiet of our own presence, we discover the value of words, the power of language to nurture our soul. We also discover the power of words that hurt us, for many of those words have become part of our internal lexicon. We are finally able to hear the words we use to talk to ourselves about ourselves.

In our loneliness we learn about the gifts of love and language. We also learn about the pains of love and language. Jesus' disappearance was an affirmation of the aloneness that is experienced as loneliness, and it prompts us to step down into the recesses of our inner selves and discover what is painful and beautiful, heart wrenching and heartwarming. A false god solves the problem of this journey, but God affirms it in the disappearance of Jesus.

In Dad's death, we were *affirmed* in our loneliness and grief, that we might explore the abyss of our own inner life and find beauty and meaning.

Jesus' disappearance was an *initiation*. He initiated a new chapter of the Messianic movement that began gaining momentum on the heels of John the Baptizer's prophetic ministry. There's a sign that hangs above the front door at my parents' house that reads: "I've got this! - God." The sign is slang for the platitude among evangelical Christians: God is in control.

The obvious problem with this platitude is how to reconcile God being in control when there is a disaster (or suffering, abject poverty, or any other calamity). One that holds to the platitude is forced to either rationalize God's role in disastrous events or overemphasize the disaster as a learning experience. The former feels like theologically contorting one's concept of God so as to not get pinned to the mat of basic sensibility. The latter is quite simply an avoidance of the conundrum (and insensitive). Both do not resolve the conflict between the implications of God saying, "I've got this!" and disaster and suffering.

A resolution may be found in Jesus' disappearance, which is an initiation. The very presence of Jesus at their table, broken bread in hand (v30), surely prompted them to remember that final meal in Jerusalem in the upper room.

Then he disappeared mid-meal.

I imagine Jesus' disappearance compelled them to follow through with the meal. For in the follow through—the actual sharing and consuming of the bread in Jesus' absence—their table became something more. It became at once the memory of that final meal with Jesus, the completion of the current meal with Jesus, and most profoundly, *the site of resurrection!* In their midst was not (only) the absence of Christ but the presence of at least two Christ-like disciples. We might say there were at least two Christs at the table.

Sharing and eating bread were not two failing disciples but the insurrectionary movement that was thought dead—the seeds for Israel's redemption. The stranger-revealed-as-Jesus mysteriously disappeared but the potency of the counter-crucifixion movement was alive.

By leaving, Jesus arrived. By disappearing, he appeared more fully in the material reality of those that embodied his memory, continuing his resurrection, and enacting his Kingdom. Jesus' disappearance is a reinterpretation of the sign that hangs over my parents' front door. God is *not* in control per se, but God *does* "got this." Through Jesus' disappearance, the disciples are initiated as the ones who *are* in control. By leaving, Jesus was handing over the responsibilities of leadership in the Kingdom to those who embody the spirit of the Eucharist, the spirit of counter-crucifixion.

When disaster struck in the form of ALS, in the sudden onslaught of confusion and suffering, in the complete inadequacy of medical intervention, it was the incarnation of God through hospitality and love that "got it." We should replace the sign with a more accurate one. It should read: *"You've* got this! – God."

In Dad's death, the death-defying, counter-crucifixion responsibilities of Jesus' ministry should be embodied and continued. In Dad's death, there is a type of *initiation*, a commissioning from God: "You've got this!" That responsibility is primarily a responsibility to offer eucharistic hospitality and love to each other and to strangers.

Jesus' vanishing affirms the aloneness of the disciples as the locus of discovering beauty and understanding. Jesus also arrives in his leaving by *initiating* a new era, one in which the disciples' are implicitly commissioned as little Christs carrying on the mission of Jesus.

In yet another way, through God's absence there is an ineffable presence. By disappearing, Jesus changes the terms of disappearance, *redefining* it not as something to be feared but as a mystery full of meaning and hope. God appears in Jesus' disappearance.

The best way to get at this *redefinition* of presence is to acknowledge the use of disappearance by Rome. Crucifixion—the whole process of incarcerating, torturing, and eventually burying—was the Empire's means of "disappearing" subjects from their own lives.

As explored earlier, crucifixion is a subtraction, a stripping of one from his communal connections that give life meaning, only to be torturously humiliated. Even though the subject is seen, he is not seen for who he is but for whom the Empire has made him: a manipulated object, hanging in pain, isolated, and hopeless. As William Cavanaugh so vividly explores in *Torture and Eucharist,* disappearance and unthinkable pain are "tools" by which the powerful manipulate the powerless. Disappearance and pain manufacture a pervasive fear under which atomized subjects are more easily controlled.[2] The mystery that surrounds the event of crucifixion is a fearful and torturous mystery.

But there is an antidote to this story. In contrast to the disappearance within crucifixion, there is the disappearance of the Crucified One that *redefines* the meaning of vanishing. After Jesus' forced disappearance, he reappears to the disciples. This not only undermines his violent, fear-inflicting crucifixion, but it affords him the opportunity to *disappear on his own terms.* The resurrection overcomes death and redefines the mystery and fear surrounding disappearance to a hope-full incarnate mystery. In other words, when Jesus disappears, so does the power of disappearance to instill fear.

Rome is not present in the objective, tangible sense, but it's always a looming presence of potential disappearance and pain. God is more present still! As the unidentified traveler on the road, then as a guest at the table, and then again as the table host, God is present in the resurrected Jesus. Further, God is present in the disappearance of Jesus, which is not a torturous manipulation, but an affirmation in the divine yet mysterious nature of hospitality and love.

In my father's dying, we all encountered the God that is experienced as mystery. The threat of death and the fear of the unknown were being *redefined* as a hope that is grounded in the mysterious presence of the Divine. Like Cleopas and his brother, we were experiencing a disappearance, but God was fully present.

VII

HOPE SECURED

They got up and returned at once to Jerusalem...
Then the two told what had happened"

— LUKE 24:33–35

22

DOING EUCHARIST

It was Saturday night and I didn't think my father would make it until Sunday. Mom's normal vigor had given way to fatigue. The sheer potency of God's presence, the miraculous sharing of wine, and the heaviness of crucifixion was a concoction for exhaustion. My mother was not alone, as we all wore the tiredness on our faces. My brothers and I agreed it was time to give Mom a chance to rest even though we would risk missing Dad's final breath. Mom agreed but requested some company.

Rick spent Saturday night with Mom and Dad. He texted all of the brothers early Sunday morning with an update. Mom was able to sleep a bit, and to our surprise, my father lay peacefully breathing in his bed. Once again, all five brothers convened at our parents' house. There was a shared understanding that this was nearly the end.

The road to Emmaus and my father's final few days of life are both Eucharistic experiences. While their journeys were quite different, they all experienced a walk toward the table that would ultimately be the site of Divine hosting. The disciples hosted Jesus, yet they became the guests at the table, accepted, valued, and affirmed. On the torturous journey through ALS, my father was also welcomed at the Eucharist table. Even further, both journeys continued after the table experience. All Eucharistic journeys continue after the consumption. The Eucharist doesn't end at the table, but in one sense *begins* there.

The only way to receive the Eucharist is to "do" the Eucharist. In other words, the Eucharist has within it an implicit call to action. To "do" the Eucharist is first to be welcomed, and then to take the risk of extending the spirit of hospitality to others. Jesus said, ". . . do this in remembrance of me" (Luke 22:19; 1 Corinthians 11:24). These words mean to "do" the Eucharist, to take the bread and wine *while remembering* its meaning. We *make memories* of the Eucharist in the very action of *doing* what makes it meaningful. Those actions are what make the Eucharist table an antithesis to crucifixion.

The table at which the Eucharist is served not only *offers symbols* that point to deeper meaning, but the table *is the meaning of the symbols* we choose to create through our embodiment of a counter-crucifixion reality.

Let me break that down a bit.

When we welcome the stranger into our lives and to our tables, we "remember" and embody the Eucharist.

When we affirm his existence, we "remember" and embody the Eucharist.

When we offer genuine, life-giving hospitality and love, we "remember" and embody the Eucharist.

Our tables welcome strangers, affirm their value, and offer them love, which is the meaning of the Eucharist. Our response to the Eucharist *is* the meaning of the Eucharist.

Dad's clothes draped over his gaunt figure and served as a reminder that crucifixion has the power to strip every ounce of strength from its victim. Torture will strip the human spirit of hope, a truth that garments cannot hide. Crucifixion, however, is not something that can only be observed. By proximity, the onlooker of such tragedy is implicated in it. The experience takes on a visceral reality, especially when the tortured is kin, biological or otherwise. The line between bodies blurs.

How would Mary, the mother of Jesus, describe her experience at the crucifixion of her son (John 19:25)? Was she suffering? Of course! Ask any parents if they feel pain when their child suffers. Dad's bony body, weak and listless, was an extension of our very own bodies. Part of me was dying an unjust death that morning.

Lying prostrate, motionless, emaciated, Dad was a reminder of death and lost hope. Now, I know that sounds horrible, even inhumane. Because it was. Unjustified suffering always is. The ravages of crucifixion are always horrible and inhumane!

But Dad was also a reminder of the antithesis of death. In the face of crucifixion, Dad risked, God risked, and conditions for being welcomed at the Eucharist table were set. Crucifixion doesn't have the last word. Death is not the final authority. Hope returned Saturday because life—not ALS, not anxiety or sleepless nights, not even crucifixion—has the last word.

In the same way that torture cannot merely be watched but is always participated in by its onlookers, eucharistic life that overcomes the power of death is participatory. Dad, Mom, and everyone who sat at the table participated in the return of ife-giving hope.

After hope returned to the disciples, they still had a road to travel. Their journey back to Jerusalem was their response to the Eucharist. Their journey back was the "remembering" of their eucharistic experience. Dad's journey wasn't over either. Our journey with Dad was not finished. Sunday was our response to the Eucharist. The final leg of these two journeys secured the hope that was once lost and had returned with bread and wine.

<hr>

EACH BROTHER, in our own way, said goodbye to Dad.

Rick and Rob reminded Dad that he was loved and that his boys were all present. "All of us are here, Dad. We love you, Dad," they said.

Randy paced while mouthing prayers. He held tightly to the memories of when he was in little league and he and Dad would play catch. He thanked God for those precious times, and he petitioned God to be gracious to Dad at the end, to welcome him over the threshold of this world of pain and terminality and into God's eternal presence.

Rocky rested his arm around Mom as a type of solidarity blanket. They both cast an affirming gaze toward Dad that said, "Together we see you, and you are loved."

I took pictures, not so much to commemorate the final moments of life or to capture the closing minutes of a chivalrous battle with ALS, but more so in an effort to slow down and connect with the potency of the moment. The focusing and zooming and clicking of the shutter gave me a cadence to follow, which helped to take notice of details, to sustain full engagement with the power of the place.

The spirit of the house, though full of tears, was hope-filled. We had witnessed miracles and come face to face with the Divine Mystery.

What struck me as particularly meaningful was how quiet the house was despite there being noise. We snacked and drank, shuffled around the living room and kitchen, and even exchanged verbal condolences. It wasn't silent, but it was quiet in the way the beach is quiet while the waves crash, the wind dances, and seagulls talk to each other. While silence is soundless, quietness is not. The noise in quietness is calm and in moderation. For noise to be quiet noise, it needs to be intentional, it needs purpose, and it needs reverence. I was struck by the reverent quietness, as it was a stark contrast to the noisiness that defines our social lives.

We live in a society that privileges extroversion. If there is a camera, it's usually pointed at an extrovert. Our leaders and heroes express extroverted qualities. We celebrate the personalities that are gregarious, loud, and confident. The cultural appetite for extroversion is so strong that it has become the predominant norm of public behavior. Consequently, everyone on some level is forced to be extroverted or deny themselves trying.

The two dominant traits of extraversion are outgoingness and a general gratification drawn from outside oneself. Extroverts prefer group settings and public conversations rather than introspection and being alone. It comes as no surprise then that our society, which privileges extroversion, also avoids silence and reflection.

There's a rich tradition of contemplative prayer in Christianity. While prayer is often thought of as talking with God, contemplative prayer is akin to silencing oneself before God. This type of prayer is counter-cultural in that it requires sustained quietness and deep listening.

Through rigid practice, I experience my true self when in contemplation. When there's no show to put on, no argument to win, no scene to stimulate, and no group to distract, there's no need for the ego to dictate my attention and actions. What I must face is myself.

The ego thrives in an extroverted world, and extroversion doesn't draw energy from being alone. Both struggle with the quiet that is fostered with the measured use of purposeful noise. As mentioned, quietness is not silence, but it is without performance and unnecessary stimulation. Quietness is ego-free noise; quietness is non-extroverted noise.

The disciples were entering back into an environment of pain and anguish. They embraced their fellow disciples in their suffering and sat quietly. Suffering does not require silence, but it demands quietness. In other words, in the face of suffering, there is no room for meaningless chatter and unintentional noise.

Let's go a step further. Extroversion and the ego serve to compound suffering. This is why answers driven by the ego—logical arguments or propositional truths, for example—are not beneficial in the presence of suffering. They are rather painful and offensive. Someone who is suffering doesn't need egotistical noise but quiet solidarity. One who is deeply in the throes of pain needs others who have been deeply in the throes of pain to be near and judicious with noise and words.

The disciples knew they were entering back into pain, as they had waded through the same pain and suffering. They were quietly present. On that Sunday, we all knew we were witnessing the final stage of crucifixion. We were in the presence of tangible suffering, and we were quiet, ourselves having journeyed through the pain with Dad. It was a quietness that is only found in an environment free of ego and extroverted chatter.

It was a contemplative and reverent quietness; it was a holy quiet.

EVEN WITH SUPPLEMENTAL OXYGEN, Dad's breathing became more challenging on Sunday morning. Each breath was but a short, abbreviated gasp, filling a fraction of his lungs. I was trying to be patient as six a.m. crept toward seven. There was nothing else to wait for, nothing else that needed attending. I quietly encouraged Dad's final breath, petitioning for final peace to set in. But death seemed held back.

Gasp. Pause. *Gasp.* Pause.

The gasps were difficult to watch, but the pauses were harder because they resembled a sustained asphyxiation. I was growing impatient that the invisible hand of time wasn't doing his job. It seemed too slow, even stalled.

Gasp. Pause. *Gasp.* Pause.

A conflict arose Sunday between my expectation for timely progress and the slowness of the eucharistic journey. The Eucharist table, like all tables that are set for guests, should mark an intentional time of inefficiency. Anyone who has hosted guests for a meal knows that meal preparation takes time, especially if it's from scratch. There are no drive-thru Eucharist experiences. Meals are slow. Eucharistic journeys—the journey toward the table and the responsive journey that follows it—are slow too. I was restless because I was in a hurry.

The bread on the table carries within it a message of slowness and inefficiency. Making bread is a patient mixing of yeast, flour, and water. Bread is a reminder that the eucharistic experience is an experience less about efficiently producing and consuming and more about the patient solidarity between guests and hosts. The bread also sustains us, the means by which we carry on without hunger after the meal. In a way, to belong, to be affirmed, to be loved by those who truly listen serves as the bread that helps us carry on with our journey long after the meal. The patient solidarity of the meal always extends beyond the table fellowship.

Wine speaks to this point as well. It is a delayed enjoyment of the toil of harvest. Months, if not years, pass before the grapes are consumed. The wine is a gentle reminder that the eucharistic meal begins long before the table is set. The meal is never measured by how quickly it transpires but by our attentiveness to the stories that develop elsewhere and intersect around the shared table. The Eucharist meal always includes the journeys that are traveled before we arrive.

The two disciples walked seven miles home on the road to Emmaus, and that was only the first portion of their eucharistic journey. Then they sat and hosted, ultimately becoming the guests at Jesus' table. The journey continued, and they traveled seven more miles back to Jerusalem. All of that walking and talking, sitting and eating, solidarity and fellowship, constituted their eucharistic journey.

My father's experience was similar. His journey was a many-month crawl. I traveled with him for only four of those days, and it was anything but efficient. Speed and efficiency are not virtues on the road to Emmaus, nor on Dad's journey to God's table. Instead, they are obstacles to the very experience of hospitality and divine presence that the Eucharist offers.

The disciples traveled in the dark on a road notoriously known for banditry. Most importantly, however, was not the risk they were taking on the road but the risk they were taking when they returned to the source of so much of their anguish. They returned to the scene of a murder, the killing of a movement, to the bloody mess that scattered so many followers of Jesus in fear. Rumors of resurrection collided with the torment of death and loss, and the disciples decidedly returned to that place.

They returned to death because they were full of hope. I'm not interested in hope that leaves the back door open as an easy escape should something go wrong. I'm also not interested in a hope that promises goosebumps and butterflies. I'm interested in the type of hope that stands me out of my seat at the very thought of death and compels me to confront it.

Jürgen Moltmann said that hope is not what calms our uneasy heart; hope *is* our uneasy heart.[1] This is the very hope that returned to the disciples at the table with Jesus. It compelled them to revisit the scene of death in Jerusalem. I'm interested in *that* kind of hope.

For Cleopas and his brother, the hope of the resurrection was not a joyful feeling that displaces their despair; it was the conviction that Rome's power to shape ideology and kill bodies was no longer permanent. Returning to Jerusalem was an act of subversion as much as it was an act of celebration. In going back to pain and death, despite the risk, they were announcing that death and control were defeated. There was no guarantee that their hope would be openly welcomed. Nonetheless, by enacting their hope—facing the risk of announcing a different reality—their hope was secured. Their journey back to Jerusalem was as important as their journey to Emmaus for securing their hope in the resurrected Christ.

Hope returned to my father when he accepted the invitation to the Divine table. The security of that hope, like the disciples' experience, would come only upon going back to death and naming a new reality. But Dad's lungs were searching for air, and the next life was near. Could he go back? There was no traveling left in his tired body. For Cleopas and his brother to face death, they needed to return to it, but Dad didn't have to travel to face death: he merely needed to wait a few more minutes.

In my notes that hour, I wrote:

> *I can feel death. It's as close as God.*
>
> *It's antagonizing me.*
>
> *I feel small but aggressive.*

Death was something Dad was about to face.

I felt "small but aggressive" staring at death from such a close distance. Its finality is its power. Death is intimidating. I felt both agitation and aggression. It was Dad's death, but it was mine to face as well. Within me was a stirring and that stirring was hope.

Dad would face death as the inevitable end to his battle with ALS, and like the two disciples, I needed to choose to face death too. My task was clear: to face death, to subvert it, and to name a new reality in the future, I needed to head back to the mess and darkness that Dad and I shared. I had to face the wounds from childhood.

As seven turned to eight that Sunday morning, time ever so slowly ticking by, Dad began gulping. The gulps were not gasps —not the machine-assisted breaths that were becoming familiar. They were something other, something worse. "Oral lurches" captures Dad's strain, akin to taking a large bite of air.

Gasp. Pause. *Gasp.* Pause. *Gulp.*

Each gulp demanded our attendance at Dad's bedside. We were ready for his final breath to mark an end to his journey.

I struggled to find my place amidst the gulping and low churn of the ventilator that assisted Dad's sleepy lungs. The rhythm of noises and movement encouraged me to settle into a reflective trance. Childhood memories, like short VHS clips, flashed before me. Was this the unraveling of memories that often accompanies grief? Why would I be going backward when Dad's life was still going forward?

Gasp. Pause. *Gasp.* Pause. *Gulp.*

One of those grainy videos flashed through my memory . . .

"Ryan, we have absolutely no tolerance for that kind of behavior!" Dad had roared. Defenseless, guilty, confused, I wept in fear. His volume escalating even further, "Do you know how this makes us look?"

Another one of those videos flashed . . .

"I'm disappointed in you," Dad had said. Small and scared, I cowered. He yelled, "This will never happen again! Do you understand me?"

The flashes of memory were not only a type of premature grief. Dad's death was triggering memories of my own small deaths from the past. I was already journeying back to revisit those dark experiences. More potently, however, his hope was inspiring in me a hope that would confront the death that I carried with me in memory.

The disciples returned to Jerusalem to contradict the prevailing reality that enabled crucifixion. I needed to journey back to disarm the many deaths that I still carried with me. "You're an adult now," says the prevailing wisdom, "what's in the past is in the past." Hope has a different opinion: darkness and pain are never permissible and must be faced. Going back to face those hurts is the only way to strip them of their determinative power. Going back is the only way to ultimately announce with hope a resurrection alternative.

I began "going back" in Dad's final hour. I will continue going back for many years, facing the darkness from parental wounds.

THE TANGIBILITY of death seems to encourage a type of manic memory. Over and over I heard Dad's request. Despite the serenity of the house and the calm of his body, my unconscious knew that in our dialogue were untapped resources to help navigate these final moments of breath, of life.

"I want you to walk with me, Ryan."

"What do you mean, Dad?"

"I want you to walk with me to the end. I trust you will go slowly. I don't want to go fast. I want to ask questions."

"Okay, Dad. Okay." I continued, "I can't promise I have many answers, Dad. But I can promise that I will tell them straight, and tell you when I don't really know."

"I just want you there with me."

"Okay, Dad. Of course."

That exchange was a sign of my father's ultimate trust in me. The gift of trust, father to a son, is a treasure. In his final hour, when the walking was finished and the end was near, I noticed in that conversation another treasure. It was a message tucked between the lines.

With the help from a song by Jon Foreman, "Learning How to Die," I received a new treasure. In that song, Foreman tells his partner he doesn't want to talk about death. His partner doesn't fear death but embraces its inevitability. As a result, she is free to use death as a learning experience. She shows both humility and courage as she stands as a pupil in the teaching presence of death. Her humility is expressed in her admission of failure; her courage is portrayed in the vulnerability required to own her ignorance, yet still pursue learning. Ultimately, Foreman's partner turns loss and death into an opportunity for learning how to live.[2]

In asking me to walk with him to the end, my father seemed to be subtly asking me: "Will you share with me your hope and teach me to face death in a way that disarms it?" Or, maybe Dad was saying, "I have questions, so will you help me learn?" And that was the new treasure that I received: All the way to death, Dad wanted to learn, and he trusted me to teach him.

Hope is a posture of learning in the face of death. Cleopas and his brother were called to this type of hope, but it began long before their dining experience with Jesus. Jesus called them to be disciples, which is to say that he called them to be students (Greek *mathetes:* student, learner) of a master craftsman. The master, of course, was the Messiah, and his craft was the inauguration of a contrasting Kingdom to the one already established. Rome used violence as a means to expand territory and as a means of controlling subjects. Jesus offered a subversive alternative to the violence and death utilized by Rome, which was an alternative of hope. His disciples were fundamentally called to be students of that hope in the face of death.

Hope is not a type of emotional tool to soothe anxieties and fears. Hope is not a perspective shift that averts attention from evil and injustice. It's not a comforting opinion that satiates restlessness and discontent. If hope were any of these, it would be precisely the numbing opium that Karl Marx pegged religion for being. Jesus taught his disciples the opposite: Hope is questioning the prevailing circumstances that cause anxiety, fear, and restlessness. Hope questions the environment where violence and death are accepted. I think this was what Dad wanted.

How does one learn from death while also questioning the conditions of death? How can one be a student and a protester, a learner and a resistor, at the same time? For the disciples, the learning process was at once acquiring new counter-crucifixion habits—hope in the face of violence, hospitality in the face of exclusion— *and* discovering the potential for crucifixion within. In terms familiar with the first band of Jesus' followers, being a disciple meant learning to resist systemic sin but also learning to root out the sin in one's own heart (Matthew 5–7). Fundamentally, hope, like discipleship itself, is an ongoing openness to learning.

Hope reminds us that we don't have answers that are forever unchanging, but as students we have strong beliefs that are always provisional. If being a student of hope is a pillar of the new Kingdom, as taught by Jesus, then being a teacher of hope is too. Discipleship has, at its very core, the concept of teaching. Of course, a student learns from a teacher, but discipleship implies that a teacher and a student co-exist in one person. This is why Jesus in his training could also send the disciples out to do a fair bit of teaching themselves (Mark 6; Luke 10).

Like an expert in any field, it's not only the knowledge that makes him brilliant but the willingness to keep learning. No one ever arrives at complete knowing. The opposite is true: the more we learn, the more we learn how little we know. Even if it was possible to learn everything there is to know today, tomorrow might bring new discoveries. There is always room to learn. What we know is necessarily provisional. That doesn't threaten our expertise or brilliance. Instead, it gives credence and depth to the brilliance because it is grounded in learning rather than static certainty.

It's not the answers that somehow soften the impact of death by getting around it and knowing what lies behind it. Instead, being fundamentally open to learning about death, which is embracing the unknowns of death as opposed to escaping them, engenders hope.

As far as I could tell, answers were not what Dad needed. "Asking questions" was not, despite a literal understanding, referring to a laundry list of queries he needed answers to before he could exit this life and enter the Next. That's not how discipleship works, that's not how hope works, and that's not how death works. "Asking questions" for my father was his language for wanting to take the posture of student and free death of its sting. The questions were not a means to answers; they were in fact a hopeful way to face death. The questions *were* the answers!

My father would never have identified with the title of "disciple," but the treasure he gave me was a lesson on how to a better one. He was teaching me the power of openness to learning, the posture of being a student. Death was at hand, and I didn't need to fight it off. Dad was teaching me to resist its sting through embracing it. He asked me to be with him, to teach him to disarm death, but ironically—and more powerfully —we became students of hope together. We were resisting crucifixion while embracing death. We were, from my perspective, disciples together.

23

WHERE'S GOD?

WE WERE AT THE END. WE HAD WALKED TO THIS POINT WITH DAD having seen hospitality extended, grace received, and hope return. I scribbled in my notes a nagging question about the end of a journey of lost hope and its final return. I thought acknowledging it by writing it down would make it go away. It didn't.

My note read:

> *Nagging question: what about conversion?*
>
> *Should I be waiting for it? Looking for it?*

While there is not much biblical precedence for deathbed conversions (Luke 23:39–43 is the strongest, though Matthew 27:44 would disagree), they serve as an important affirmation of two pillars of evangelical theology. They reinforce the belief that the primary goal of salvation is admittance into heaven.

Timing is not a factor, which is why it's never too late to be saved. It also supports the significance and benefit of Divine grace. Grace has a pardoning effect on the entirety of one's sins and sinfulness.

End-of-life conversions also have a powerful role in the evangelical imagination. They are the Starbucks eggnog latte of religious conversion: everything desirable and delicious in one experience. All that we have grown to expect in a conversion experience is concentrated at the end of life. It's the perfect fix for our evangelical religious cravings. However, like the eggnog latte, everything unhealthy is also concentrated into one experience. A guilt-free ticket to heaven is obtained without any of the work. It's all glory—no fear and trembling—and no risk (Philippians 2:12). The holy grail of Christianity is obtained, none of the change required.

What is religious conversion without transformation? What good is conversion without a sustained confrontation with oneself over time? It makes me wonder if conversion itself has become, in the evangelical imagination, a type of idol.

An idol is a product of our own making to protect us from what is real. In the classic, religious sense, an idol is an object of worship.[1] But an idol is also a cultural term. It's a reference to a famous person that's highly revered or desired.

In the first concept, the object does not have to be tangible. So long as we fashion them—institutions, events, or even a goal— and have imparted divine significance to them, they are idols. This type of idolatry is about creating "false gods" that meet my need for security or comfort or control. In other words, it says as much about my needs as it does about the god I worship.

In the second concept, we do not so much idolize the celebrity as we idolize an imagined connection with him or her. A picture of the idol is the portal through which I can imaginarily enter into the life of that famous person or vice versa. This kind of idolatry is as much about me as the celebrity because through it I create a fictional reality that is more desirable than the true reality I am trapped in.

Both concepts of idolatry enable attachment to one thing (an idol) as a protection or escape from the confrontation of another thing (myself). Idols are so alluring because they're effective, and they're so effective because in their familiarity they hide in plain view. If the idol persists long enough, it becomes itself the new "real." This is perhaps what (end-of-life) conversion has become to modern Evangelicalism.

My appetite for Dad's conversion was less about heavenly admission than it was about me not wanting to cope with what was real: the grief and uncertainty that is inevitable after death and loss. I was in need of certainty, knowing without doubt that Dad was heaven-bound and I was somehow protected from grief.

I realized that even in the face of so much beauty and Divine presence, welling up within me was an idolatrous desire in the final moments of Dad's life. I still had a craving for a conversion experience, a type of repentant moment for Dad. The more I tried to ignore it—jotting it down in my notes and hoping it would go away—the more it echoed in my head. I wasn't craving Divine grace for which I had already witnessed in abundance. I was craving an event that would magically wipe away the scars of a painful past and the inevitable wounds of loss that would come. And, evidently, I still had an appetite for what God might offer my father in terms of last minute, heavenly entrance.

In my father's final hour, I was confronted with the hard truth that I sometimes worship an idolatrous god that threatens to stand before the God that was truly present. In other words, I sometimes prefer a divine being that works sensationally and quickly rather than be present and patient.

Spiritual writer Richard Rohr and others have challenged me to "gently hold endings" that are without clean closure.[2] Part of the virtue of hope is to live without needing the satisfaction of "living happily ever after" (which we know is really the way only fairy tales end).

What Rohr means in part is that hope is to live without the idol of conversion. Deathbed conversion is a type of ultimate closure and certainty. But it also exposes the possibility of an idolatrous need for control. My reality is full of unknowing and uncertainty. To live with hope is to find satisfaction in the "loose ends" knowing that it's not contingent on fulfilling my desire for closure but in embracing, and even confronting, the world that is out of my control.

Hope, in this small way, is the pushback to my tendency toward idolatrous control, my fetishizing of a confessional event at the last minute of life (that I encouraged, facilitated, or even cajoled). Hope's return at the end of Dad's life demanded that I embrace the messy uncertainty that is the final moment of living.

I didn't see a connection between them at the time, but only later I realized how my notes related to each other:

Nagging question: what about conversion?

Should I be waiting for it? Looking for it?

Immediately after, but with a big space between them, I wrote:

Hope! Mom and Dad's house is full of tears and hope.

Not as I expected. There's a peace here.

Can't be long before Dad lets go.

It appears that each note captures two different experiences, the former about conversion and the latter about hope. What I was observing, however, was not two disparate phenomena; instead, they were related, for the latter was the undoing of the former. Hope amidst the anguish, and the peace of Divine hospitality in the face of crucifixion, were the undoing of the idol of conversion.

My fetish, my idol, would not mark the end of Dad's life.

God's presence would mark the end.

Hope would mark the end.

WESLEY PALMER WAS my friend who laughed the hardest and suffered the most. We would meet almost every morning for coffee and conversation at the food bank. We chose the food bank because it was across the street from where he stayed, which was the abandoned bank building on Main Street. Wesley was homeless and addicted to numbing his pain. With a sixth-grade education and no chance for employment, he had given up on all but one aspect of his life: serving others who share his suffering. He volunteered every day at the food bank and helped every Sunday at the soup kitchen.

Wesley told me all about his dreams. There was one that would change each time but with a recurring storyline. He dreamt he died and went to heaven, and upon arrival, an angel asked him his name. After searching for Wesley Sanders in the *Book of Life*, the angel shook her head and apologized, "I'm sorry, Wesley, your name's not here." After looking over it one more time, she said, "Wait! Here it is, scribbled at the bottom. Come on in."

As Wesley felt relief, he also felt a sense of loss. Searching for where these conflicting feelings came from, he looked around, confused. Then he noticed others who looked just like him, beaten up by life yet denied entrance. To his left and right, well into the distance, his neighbors stood, having heard the news: "You can't enter."

"Thanks, ma'am," he said to the angel and pointed at his neighbors, "but I'll stay out here with them." Then Wesley would laugh his big, roaring laugh and always make the same comment, "Isn't that where Jesus'd be? I'll stay with Jesus."

The dream doesn't highlight whether we have a choice in our eternal future but instead it challenges our very understanding of heaven. And it does this indirectly, with a genuine adherence to the portrayal of Jesus in scripture.

The dream forces us into an imaginative predicament between heaven and Jesus. We're stuck between our concept of heaven and the new concept of "outside-heaven" where Jesus chooses to be. Both are appealing, which loosens up our epoxy-like adherence to heaven as a result of a singular, clear choice about eternal destinations. Even further, the burden of being in the middle has a surprise effect: it reduces the fear of heaven's opposite.[3]

The dream also disrupts our concept of heaven "out there" as a contrast to the world "down here". What's happening outside heaven to which Wesley is drawn? The hurting are being served, and the oppressed are being shown compassion. He chooses to continue the habits of service that marked his life "down here." What's happening outside seems to be taken straight out of the Gospels.[4] Jesus' incarnational ministry was a heavenly engagement with the world "down here." The dream reveals that our desire for heaven risks disengaging us from this world, relieving us of serving in heavenly ways.

We might call the place Wesley chooses to stay a "heaven outside of heaven" because that's where Jesus is and it's where heavenly things occur. It happens to be the same "place" Mother Teresa also preferred. She's quoted as saying, "If I ever become a saint—I will surely be one of 'darkness.' I will continually be absent from heaven—to light the light of those in darkness on earth."[5]

Some may question: *Is this biblical?* Yes and no. Yes, it's biblical because it *is* the biblical narrative that we are all familiar with. But "heaven outside of heaven" is not just in the Bible, chapter and verse—it's theologically consistent with the very concept of the incarnation when heaven broke open and God descended to Earth as a child. The birth of Christ was a divinely instituted reality that we can call "heaven outside of heaven."

Wesley's dream resonated deeply with a profound pastoral insight I learned from Jürgen Moltmann. Moltmann says the sufferer doesn't ask "Why, God?" as if to need a rationale for pain. Instead, the suffering asks, "Where's God?"[6] The power in this question is the point that when we are in pain, location is more important than reason. The suffering person always needs proximity—especially Divine proximity—more than justification or explanations.

"Where's God?"

Cleopas and his brother got their answer to that question: "On the road with you and at your table."

Dad received his answer as well: "In your home, massaging your feet, holding your hands, rubbing your legs, weeping, praying, whispering affirmations. And at the table."

There is no "out there" in the face of death; there is no other place to desire. The most precious truth is that heaven comes down and is in the very midst of the suffering—in solidarity between creature and Creator, humanity and God, flesh and the Divine.

The "heaven outside of heaven" is in the very presence of the suffering. Wesley knew that. I was also learning that too. I think we were all in our own unique way letting go of heavenly desires so that we might truly enter with Dad in the heaven all around us.

WE WERE alert and paying attention to every detail. My father's skin began to empty of pigment. His blood retreated toward its home, his heart. His breaths became shorter and softer. His lower lip drooped like a lazy Salvador Dali clock, and his face was gaunt and lifeless. Dad's body was no longer his, for his spirit was merely loaning it for a moment or two more.

We were in the final moments of what had become a powerful journey of taking risks, being vulnerable, and facing death. The six of us were tense with anticipation of the final breath of Dad's life.

Death is portrayed so dramatically in film. Big, empty breaths, screams, hands grasping chests, futile swallows, eyes rolling. Even the less dramatic endings are dramatized with dialogue, lighting, music, and exaggerated reactions from bystanders. I didn't expect Dad's death to be like something from a Bruce Willis film, but I did half expect it to be like an old Western—dramatized dialogue, sun setting in the background. It was neither of these.

It was a final breath like any breath. No drama.

A breath, then silence.

We were all around Dad, discerning from the pigment of his skin and the deep calmness of his spirit that the end was right there, inches away. There was a cadence to the room. Dad's chest would gently rise, the oxygen ventilator would follow with a chirp, his chest would fall, and then there was a pause. It was predictable. But right at the end, the pause became longer.

Chest rise, chirp, chest descend. Pause. Pause.

And then there wasn't a rise, a chirp, a pause.

Pause. And nothing else. A void of movement. The pause became something more, something deeper. Something permanent.

Mom said through her tears, "Is that it?"

"Yes, Mom," several of us said in unison.

All six of us were leaning in, looking, attending closely to that final breath. And now we were looking at breathlessness. Like kids peering over the brooder box at the farm store trying to get a good view of the baby chicks, we were looking at life that was born only a few days before. In his suffering, and despite his crucifixion, Dad was born anew. Life emerged that was hidden for so long behind a shell of hurt and fear. And it finally cracked.

We were not looking at death but life, not a last breath but in many ways one of the first true breaths of freedom that Dad had had in many decades. We were witness to a father and a marriage that were only recently born.

Night befell my father's life last December with the diagnosis of Amyotrophic Lateral Sclerosis. All light, all possibility, all hope of recovery was lost. Then something else happened from within. The light within grew brighter, more fully revealing the richness of hues that were once undisclosed. It was not merely the circumstance of night that allowed us from the outside to perceive an inner light. There was a freedom and healing from within that illuminated Dad's life more brilliantly as death approached. Like stained glass, the light within revealed my father's beauty, the colors of hope shown.

Dad's lifeless body was brilliantly colorful, having succumbed to the crucifixion of ALS, but having become illuminated by the closeness of a God that risked on his behalf and ultimately freed him through hospitality and love.

There was an intentional break after we confirmed Dad's death. No one rushed to their phones; no one grew restless. We all embraced, we cried, and we followed Dad's lead and rested.

Death is final rest.

It's the final call we all share—the call to be fully still.

It's not fundamentally a portal to the afterlife no matter how hard we work to console our anxieties with thoughts of heavenly teleportation. The truth is we don't know what happens immediately after one dies, but we do know that rest sets in, a deep indwelling of calm and peace. And in this way, deep restfulness, even final rest, is a type of life in itself. You could say that something is created in the motionless and peaceful moment of calm. It's dynamic and holy.

The Divine Creator set a precedent for the creativity and holiness of rest. God rested as part of creation, as was recorded by the author of Genesis. It was the seventh day of creation, not a complimentary afterthought to the six days of creative activity. Without the seventh day, creation is not complete. It was designated as a day with holy significance, sharing in the very likeness of the Divinity (Genesis 1:1–2:3).

Sabbath rest produces a type of creative completion, a necessary though perhaps not material "component" to the creative process. By being the finality of creation, it becomes for creation the means by which holiness might be detected as present all along the way in the creative process. Holiness is not only that which follows creation, but is within and throughout it.

Rest is not so much a stoppage of all activity but the active awareness of the holiness within all creative activity. This is why rest is a type of life: it literally brings to life within us the palpability of Divine presence, the immanence of the holy in ourselves and our environment. Without rest—without Sabbath—this awareness goes missing. Death is a final life-giving Sabbath; it's the paramount moment of the closeness of divinity. For Dad, the Sabbath rest that set in when his heart slept was both a confirmation of the closeness of God throughout his fight with ALS and an appropriate completion to it.

Sabbath rest also reminds us that life is a gift and in that life, God is present. Rest is at once revelatory and redeeming, revealing and freeing. This is what Cleopas and his brother experienced at the table hosted by Jesus the Christ. Divine closeness was revealed; liberation from the bondage of lost hope and death was tangible. The two disciples experienced perhaps the most profound truth for a world that never stops: there is deep rest at the Eucharist table. The Eucharist meal is a sabbatical resistance against crucifixion.

My farther lay still, deeply resting, which was the appropriate posture to finish his eucharistic journey. The Sabbath promised at the Eucharist table, concentrated in the syringe-of-hope, was here in full, in completion.

Perpetual Sabbath had befallen his weary body. In a way, he was faithfully responding to his final call of life: not to die, but to rest well, rest deeply, to be perfectly still. It was there, on that bed, still and peaceful, while the world continued on, while we all wept and embraced and mourned, that Dad received the gift of Sabbath rest. That gift, which is a gift of freedom, is a permanent gift—one to be permanently received and perpetually accepted with gratitude.

Dad died grateful. In our tears, with Dad, we were grateful too.

Not toward death but toward life, Dad's Eucharist journey was complete.

2 4

FAREWELL

Death is not clean.

And the timing is always bad, it seems.

We try to sanitize the process, manage it, and make it predictable. When there's too much intervention, too much control, finding meaning is almost impossible.

The mess is where the beauty is found.

The epitome of controlling death is to hide it entirely. The loss —and in the end, the challenge of the meaning-making process —is compounded by not fully experiencing the death. The antithesis to hiding death is to be fully present with little intervention. I did not set out to experience Dad's death so closely and with such fullness, but because I did, I have been able to discover heaps of meaning.

The process that I witnessed, the crucifixion that I watched, became beautiful, which is why I have begun to think of it as Simone Weil says in *Gravity and Grace,* a "precious thing." It was a journey from ugliness to beauty, from lost hope to secure hope, from death to life. What began with the trauma of crucifixion ended with hospitality, hope, and life-giving rest. This story captures Dad's transformation through vulnerability, me facing my own idols, and our encounter with the God that bends down and offers hope in the midst of suffering. With help from the Emmaus Road story, I tried to make sense of the rugged terrain, to grieve, and to honor the story that was within me and begging to be released. Only now can I say that the story of Dad's death is a story of *hope*.

This is not a conclusion, as if Dad's death needs a decisive ending. As I have said, this journey has been about discovery, and what I discovered was a light within my father that needed a little dark to shine. As many have rightfully stated about death, my father lives on through his legacy. The stories we continue to tell about his life celebrate and reinforce that legacy. But I want to add to that truism: Dad's *dying* also lives on. What I have learned through his *dying* lives on in my life by way of my embodiment of the truths that I discovered by being present at his bedside and reflecting on the notes I took along the way.

This is not at all a closing to Dad's story but an invitation to continue finding meaning on the journey of life, which is always at once a journey toward death and, potentially, a journey toward the Eucharist. Consequently, this closing is more a farewell.

A farewell is a bid for healthy traveling; the end of this book marks the end of one adventure, but it also marks the beginning of many others. To offer a farewell is also to offer a type of benediction, bestowing a blessing, but also sending with it a task for the journey ahead.

I bid you farewell. Find life amidst death, offer hope where it is lost, and remember that hospitality welcomes the stranger and the Divine Mystery to the same table where all receive bread and wine, affirmation, and love.

Also, farewell, Dad.

I love you.

EPILOGUE

Silence is the best anticipation of the future world.

— HENRI NOUWEN

It's impossible to miss: "MARK V FASANI BUILDING NORTH." All capital block letters fastened to a cream stucco backdrop, fifteen feet off the ground on the south-facing wall. Those letters, the emblazoned commemoration, hover over a major thoroughfare at Wilson C. Riles Middle School. The wall bearing Dad's name is supported by two steel columns painted blue to match the letters, propping up the architectural tonnage and the contradiction of a man they represent.

The geometry of the architecture, even the colors, are a type of cushion to absorb the chaos of preteens shuffling from class to class. But the students don't only walk under an overhang on a school building, oblivious to its commemoration; they walk into a shadowy understory of a forest, albeit an urban forest, searching for meaning and beauty amidst the blandness of cream stucco and the banal gray of concrete. Nothing of the landscape suggests that adventure is found here. Nothing suggests they will discover native, wild truths about themselves, their purpose, life itself, save for one thing: the emblazoned name of MARK V FASANI.

The students don't know who Mark V. Fasani is, and they likely don't care. Perhaps they don't know they care. Within them is a bit of wildness and wonder, and when they stand under Dad's name, they stand with me next to Dad's bedside. From that bedside, I took one risky step into the shadows of Dad's life— that step precipitated an adventure that is now this book. The students are only one courageous step from an adventure of discovery. Dad's name, and the shadow it casts over the students, silently encourages them to step into the dark under-stories of life and discover hospitality and forgiveness, love and hope. Not only Dad's teaching career, but his life and his dying, are commemorated on that stucco wall. Dad's hope, my hope, are bolted on that wall, each letter a reminder and an invitation.

I drove to see those two buildings. School was out, so I made like a student and pretended to walk to class under the twelve-inch letters and between the blue steel columns. Unlike the cacophony of schoolchildren that usually fills the corridor, the scratching of my own heels on the concrete were the only sounds. I stopped and looked up at Dad's name. It was silent. I rehearsed some of our conversations from those final four days.

Almost a year has passed, but I was back at his bedside. "I can't promise I have many answers, Dad. But I can promise that I will tell them straight and tell you when I don't really know."

I remember his very response: "I just want you there with me."

I began to cry. "I miss you, Dad."

There was no response, of course; I was talking to stucco and steel and memories.

There never will be a response, Ryan, I thought. My nose joined my eyes in swelling. I wiped it with my sweater sleeve. (Remember, I was making like a middle schooler.)

I tried consoling myself by replying as if I were Dad: "I just want you there with me."

Silence.

I held onto those words. They were not a harness that saved me from falling into the silence; rather, they pulled me further into it. There was something there . . . something more. The silence wasn't empty; it was full. I said it again, "I just want you there with me."

An invitation! Dad's silence, accentuated by the silence on campus that day, the silence of blue letters and the wall, the silence of the sky above, and the silence of the shadow below join together as an invitation. Dad's silence will always be an invitation to take a risk and be together, to be vulnerable. As I stood under Dad's name—silent, cold, concrete in every direction—I imagined a future where we are indeed together, not in some utopian union, but together again, honest about our weaknesses and our wounds. Dad's silence will always be an invitation into solidarity. I can't imagine a better future.

Dad's silent name fastened to that wall, "MARK V FASANI," is not for students a mere moniker but a story, an invitation, a promise that if they risk, they will discover, like me, a future of hope.

238

ACKNOWLEDGMENTS

On one hand, this book is still the tear-soaked notes from my father's bedside. Without his invitation to come close while he was vulnerable, none of these notes would have been scratched down. Dad is *the* person who deserves my deepest gratitude. Thank you, Dad, for inviting me along.

On the other hand, people don't write books; communities write books. This story would be a bumbling mess without many brilliant friends and family members who helped me make sense of my thoughts and helped me put words to my stories.

Eric and Nathan, thank you for diving in when this project was barely intelligible.

Rick, thank you for your help, despite my insensitive request to weigh in on my writing while you were dealing with Dad's loss.

Amalea and Carol, thank you both dearly for combing through this story and picking out the stubborn mistakes.

Mom, I hope this book serves as a sign of my thankfulness for your constant cheerleading. You cheered me on from the first hint of a book-length dream when all I had were a few long reflections. You are, and probably always will be, my biggest fan. Thank you.

Viki and Trudy, thank you for teaching me to look upon the mundane with a sacred lens.

Allison, without your skillful feedback this book would be average at best. Thank you for your help. And for the encouraging words.

Derek and Klug Publishing, it's been a joy. Let's do it again.

Launch Team. You know who you are. If you told one friend about this little story, thank you for getting this book to the world.

Above all, I am deeply thankful to my wife, Bohdana, and my kids, Katahdin, Ahanu, Chenoah, and Adele (Nalei). Thank you for your patience while Papa typed, and typed, and typed some more. Even more, I'm grateful for your support in the grieving process I underwent after Nonno's death.

ABOUT THE AUTHOR

Ryan Fasani is a pastor, writer, and farmer, which is to say he tries to point people toward the holy, sees important things and jots them down, and believes Wendell Berry is a saint.

He lives on a farm with his wife, four kids, and seven milk goats. He's currently starting a church-planting and ministry incubator in Washington State and loves coaching soccer.

He blogs daily about creativity, calling, and social change at **ryanfasani.blog**.

If you want a behind-the-scenes look at *Consuming Hope*, or if you want to be the first to hear about Ryan's next memoir, sign up for his newsletter at **consuminghope.com**.

Instagram: **/ryanfasani**
Facebook: **@realryanfasani**

NOTES

2. AUTUMN

1. Lutwig Wittgenstein, *Tractatus Logico-Philosophicus,* trans. C. K. Ogden (New York: Hardcourt, Brace & Company, Inc., 1922), 74.
2. Parker Palmer, *Let Your Life Speak: Listening for the Voice of Vocation,* (San Francisco: Jossey-Bass, 2000). The concept of autum, as it relates to the seasons of life, was inspired by Palmer's use of it in this book.

3. DIGNITY

1. Wikipedia, "Lou Gehrig," accessed February 16, 2020, https://en.wikipedia.org/wiki/Lou_Gehrig#Death.
2. Wikipedia, "Amyotrophic Lateral Sclerosis," accessed February 16, 2020, https://en.wikipedia.org/wiki/Amyotrophic_lateral_sclerosis#Name. The information I include about ALS was gathered mostly from pamphlets my mother brought home from doctors' appointments. I confirmed the specifics with the article cited here.
3. Paul Tillich, *The Courage to Be,* (New Haven: Yale University Press, 2004).
4. Kester Brewin, *Getting High: A Savage Journey to the Heart of Getting High,* (New York: Vaux Books, 2016). Josh is a master compost builder, which, of course, is a controlled process of decay. If there is an authority on decomposition—at least as it relates to death and its regenerative potentials on the farm—it is Josh. I found out later that he came to some of his conclusions about decay and death with the help of Brewin's theological memoir.

4. CHRISTMAS

1. Todd Burpo and Lynn Vincent, *Heaven is for Real* (Nashville: Thomas Nelsen, 2010).

10. BENT DOWN

1. Robert Bly, *A Little Book on the Human Shadow,* (San Francisco: HarperOne, 1988).
2. I was turned on to this concept of Sigmund Freud's by Peter Rollins, *Insurrection: To Believe Is Human To Doubt, Divine* (New York: Simon and Schuster, 2011), 85.
3. Michael E. Lodahl, *When Love Bends Down: Images of the Christ Who Meets Us Where We Are,* (Kansas City: Foundry Publishing, 2006). I first heard Dr. Lodahl speak of a bent-down Jesus at a chapel service at Point Loma Nazarene University in 2001.

11. SPACE BETWEEN US

1. Peter Rollins, *The Orthodox Heretic: And Other Impossible Tales,* (Brewster, MA: Paraclete Press, 2009).
2. Palmer, *Let Your Life Speak.*

12. CONVERSION

1. Mother Teresa, *Come Be My Light: The Private Writings of the Saint of Calcutta,* ed. Brian Kolodiejchuk, (New York: Random House, 2007).

13. CONFESSION

1. Brené Brown, *Daring Greatly: How the Courage to be Vulnerable Transforms the Way We Live, Love, Parent, and Lead,* (New York: Avery, 2015).

14. INVITATION

1. Emmanuel Levinas, *Otherwise than Being: Or Beyond Essence,* trans. By Alphonso Liungis, (Pittsburgh: Duquesne University Press, 1998.

15. REDEMPTION

1. Plumb, "Lord I'm Ready Now," track #2 on *Exhale,* Word Records and Curb Records, 2015, CD. Jon Foreman, "Learning How to Die," track #1 on *Winter,* Lowercase People, Credential, 2008, CD.
2. Bodhipaksa, "We are all formed of frailty and error; let us reciprocally pardon each other's folly," *Wildmind Meditation* (blog). March 1, 2016. Wildmind.org. Voltaire's exact words are, "We are all formed of frailty and error; let us reciprocally pardon each other's folly." I found this quote while reading about the artwork of Ukrainian sculptor, Alexander Milov, and his famous sculpture that was on display at the Burning Man festival in Nevada 2015.
3. Levinas, *Ethics and Infinity,* trans. by Richard A. Cohen, (Pittsburgh: Duquesne University Press, 1985) 85.
4. Martin Buber, *I and Thou,* (New York: Touchstone, 1971). Buber calls this encounter an "I-thou" relationship. I heartily recommend his book.
5. The most common biblical reference for this understanding of redemption comes from Romans 3:23-25: "For all have sinned and fall short of the glory of God, and all are justified freely by his grace through the redemption that came by Christ Jesus. God presented Christ as a sacrifice of atonement, through the shedding of his blood—to be received by faith."
6. For example, the Exodus of the Israelites from slavery is a predominant Old Testament redemption story. Exodus 6:7 specifically refers to retaking possession of the people of Israel.

16. SLUMBER

1. Theologian Paul Tillich is often given credit for saying, "The opposite of faith is not doubt, it's certainty."
2. Internet Encyclopedia of Philosophy, s.v. "Phaedo," by Plato (accessed January 6, 2020), https://www.iep.utm.edu/phaedo/.

17. I LOVE YOU

1. Henri Nouwen, *The Dance of Life: Weaving Sorrows and Blessings into One Joyful Step,* (Notre Dame: Ave Maria Press, 2006), 163.

19. CONSUMING HOPE

1. Brother Lawrence, *Practicing the Presence of God,* (Eastford, CT: Martino Fine Books, 2016).

20. REVELATION

1. St. Augustine, *Confessions,* trans. by Henry Chadwick, (Oxford: Oxford Press, 2009), 3.
2. Josh McDowell, *Evidence that Demands a Verdict: Historical Evidence for the Christian Faith, Volume I,* (Nashville: Thomas Nelson, 1972). For those interested, my family later had the much anticipated eight-hundred page, two-volume set, which was combined in *The New Evidence That Demands A Verdict: Evidence I & II Fully Updated in One Volume To Answer The Questions Challenging Christians in the 21st Century* (Nashville: Thomas Nelson, 1999).
3. Emmanuel Levinas quoted in John D. Caputo, *What Would Jesus Deconstruct?: The Good News of Postmodernity for the Church,* (Grand Rapids: Baker Academic, 2007), 44.
4. Thomas Merton, *New Seeds of Contemplation,* (New York: New Directions Books,1961). This concept is found throughout Thomas Merton's work. I recommend, as an introduction to Merton and his understanding of contemplation and the contemplative life.

21. (DIS)APPEARANCE

1. Henri Nouwen, "On Loneliness, Part 6," interviewed by Fr. John Catoir, St. Jude Media Ministry, May 2, 2019, accessed at https://www.youtube.com/watch?v=9RLLmu0GddA. Similar concepts are taken up in Nouwen, *The Wounded Healer: Ministry in Contemporary Society,* (New York: Doubleday, 1972).
2. William Cavanaugh, *Torture and Eucharist: Theology, Politics, and the Body of Christ,* (Oxford: Blackwell, 1998).

22. DOING EUCHARIST

1. Jürgen Moltmann, *Theology of Hope: On the Ground and Implications of a Christian Eschatology,* trans. by James W. Leitch, (Minneapolis: Fortress, 1993), 21.

2. Jon Foreman, "Learning How to Die," track #1 on *Winter,* Lowercase Records and People Recordings, Credential, 2008, CD.

23. WHERE'S GOD?

1. The golden calf from Exodus 32.
2. Richard Rohr, *Job and the Mystery of Suffering: Spiritual Reflections,* (Chestnut Ridge, NY: Crossroad, 1998). Also, see Richard Rohr, *Falling Upward: Spirituality for the Two Halves of life* (San Francisco: Jossey Bass, 2011).
3. I'm *not* suggesting there's not a hell where people endlessly suffer or are forever separated from God as much as I'm pointing to the fact that Wesley's dream frees us from the unnecessary burden of fearing hell and thereby desire a heavenly escape.
4. Literally open up any of the four Gospels and start reading. Within a chapter you'll run into Jesus showing compassion. Or, read Luke 4:14-21, which is Jesus's pronouncement of his earthly ministry.
5. Teresa, *Come Be My Light.*
6. Jürgen Moltmann, *Jesus Christ: For Today's World,* trans. Margaret Kohlin (New York: Fortress, 1995), 30–34. I owe a great deal to one of my seminary professors, Dr. M. Douglas Meeks, for introducing me to Moltmann, and specifically to Dr. Meeks's insistence on the primary question, "Where's God?" in the midst of suffering.

Made in the USA
Las Vegas, NV
18 July 2021

26653990R00159